Family Minutes

Proven Steps to Successful Parenting and Stronger Marriages—One Minute at a Time

Mark Merrill

Foreword by Trent Dilfer

FAMILY
FIRST
PUBLISHING

Published by Family First, Inc., P.O. Box 2882, Tampa, Florida 33601

ISBN 0-972-464-80-8

Printed in the United States of America

To my wife, Susan—my sweet_____(it's our secret!)

I adore you! Thanks for teaching me how to be a better husband and dad. I'm still learning!

To my children,

Megan—my sweet girl
Emily—my baby girl
Marky—my big man

Who loves you the most ever? Daddy!

To Mom and Dad,

Mom—you taught me that family was most important.

Dad—because of you, "perseverance" is my middle name!

To my brothers, Bill and Bob—

thanks for being my best friends.

ACKNOWLEDGEMENTS

While this book is based on a compilation of *Family Minute* radio scripts written over the past several years, the source of much of that content comes from fourteen years of marriage, thirteen years of parenting and forty-four years of being a son and brother.

Our *Family Minute* radio program was put on the U.S. map in a big way because of the sales skills of Amy Flowers. As a result of that success, we are now able to offer you this book. Patty Erickson, the book project manager, is the one who made it all happen. What you are holding in your hand is a product of her hard work. Behind every good book there is a great editor. Rochelle Schweizer has been just that. Nancy Jergins, a very talented writer, has spent many hours helping me put my thoughts on paper and giving them her creative touch. And David Dunham, my guide and consultant on this book, has already inspired me to start several more books.

Our Family First team—Marlene Nikolich, my loyal assistant; Charmayne Balames, my smiling typist; Kim Leamon our *Family Minute* radio program coordinator; Barbara Hall, our numbers cruncher; Felicia Liddell, who compassionately responds to the needs of our constituents; Adam Swetlik and Bryan Davis, two young men with good ideas and promising futures; and, David Brownlee, my partner at Family First—all know that this book, and everything else we do, is a team effort!

HOW TO USE THIS BOOK

While this book is designed to be a daily reader, one of its more important features is that you are able to access information when you need it. On the corner of each page you'll find a subject heading, and a complete subject index is listed in the back of the book, where you'll find the following categories:

Parenting
Discipline
Fatherhood
General Parenting
Grandparents
Motherhood
Parenting Teens
Single Parenting

Marriage
General Marriage
Husbands
Wives

Family Life
Character
Elderly Care
Family Health

Family Time
Finances
Holidays
Inspirational
Kids and Culture
Relationships
Self Improvement
Single Adults

So if you are struggling with a particular area in your life, please feel free to jump ahead and access those readings which might help meet that need. I've also included space on the bottom of each page under the words "My Thoughts." Since learning and communication is a two-way street, I hope that you'll respond to what you read. Maybe what you read will bring to light an area in your life that you need to pay greater attention to. Or maybe there is something you would like your spouse to read. Whatever your thoughts—write them down. That's usually the first step to remembering what you've read and perhaps making a change in your life.

FOREWORD

I was privileged to quarterback the winning team in Super Bowl XXXV. Was it a thrill? Absolutely. More than anyone could ever imagine.

But the thrill of a Super Bowl victory doesn't last for long.

What does last, however, is my family.

After the sportswriters have written their last words about me, after my teammates have taken their last instructions from me, and after the fans have given their last cheers for me, I will still have what matters most. I will have my family—but only if I make them my priority.

My job as an NFL quarterback takes everything I have to give—and more. And there are days when I walk in the door at home and feel like I have nothing left. But that's when, as a father and a husband, I have to rise above what's best for me and act on what I know is best for my family.

One thing I have learned in life is that I can't do everything, nor can I know everything. I depend on my coaches when I'm playing football, and I rely on my manager and accountant to make sure that my business affairs and finances are in great shape. The same thing is true about raising a family. I don't have all the answers on how to be a great dad or a loving husband. That's why I depend on family experts like Mark Merrill for advice and counsel when it comes to my family. Mark has put together a powerful tool that will help us all build stronger and healthier families. This book will require only a minute of your time a day, but the impact you feel may very well last a lifetime.

Trent Dilfer

Winning Quarterback, Super Bowl XXXV

INTRODUCTION

If you're like me, you probably don't have a lot of time. And the last thing you want to do is wade your way through a thick book that makes a heavy demand on your time.

Well, this book will only take a minute. Literally. I've planned it precisely with the busy person in mind. Maybe you have young kids or a demanding job or an extended family to care for. Don't worry. Read this book for one minute each day. My hope is that you'll find it encouraging, challenging, enlightening and perhaps even a little fun.

I've tried to provide little nuggets here that can help you in your life. But if you are struggling with a particularly difficult issue, please don't be afraid to get some professional help. Find a counselor who values the family and is sensitive and willing to help you.

I hope you enjoy reading this as much as I enjoyed writing it.

Mark Merrill
Tampa, Florida
Tuesday, October 7, 2002

DREAMS

Now that we are in the future—the 21st century—what lies ahead for us?

A hundred years ago airplanes were just a theory. The car was merely a dream. And a laptop computer—that was inconceivable! But what seemed impossible then is as common now as buggy whips and buttonhooks were in 1900. Thank goodness people like Orville Wright, Henry Ford and Bill Gates didn't take no for an answer. And from their examples, we should encourage our kids to dream beyond what they can see. Einstein believed you could lose touch with tomorrow by believing in the limitations of today.

This new century belongs to our children. Just imagine the possibilities.

MY THOUGHTS:

_____

_____

_____

FAMILY MINUTES

HEALTHY NEW YEAR

Want to know how you can get the New Year off to a healthy start?

Make a resolution to go to church. Researchers are finding it's good for the body as well as the soul. Studies at the Johns Hopkins School of Medicine found that going to worship services on a regular basis is a big boost for your overall health. Another study discovered that religious commitment helps ward off cancer. And yet one more bit of research found that regular churchgoers live longer than those who don't attend.

So make a resolution that will make your new year happy and healthy.

MY THOUGHTS:

GETTING FOCUSED

Does your family have a focus for the New Year?

Having a focus can make your family more connected and productive. Try this. Call a family meeting and brainstorm about areas you'd like to focus on over the coming year. Maybe it's having more fun together as a family or serving others through good deeds. You might want to concentrate on being kind to each other or growing in your faith. Choose one focus and boil it down to one word like fun, serving, kindness or faith. Then post the word around the house and have monthly activities to bring your focus into full view.

If you have a focus, you will be able to see more clearly how you are doing as a family.

MY THOUGHTS:

_____

_____

_____

WRITTEN GOALS

Have you ever put your goals in writing?

A famous Harvard study followed the progress of students who had written out their goals while still in college. Years later those students were found to be more satisfied with their lives and more successful than those who had not put their goals in writing. So to help achieve your dreams, write them down. First, be specific with your goals. Next, write out three things you can do to reach each one. And, finally, evaluate your progress at least every year.

Start writing to help make your dreams a reality.

MY THOUGHTS:

HARSH WORDS HURT

Are your words hurting your children?

The poet Longfellow said, "A torn jacket is soon mended; but hard words bruise the heart of a child." Do you know how much your children want your love and approval? No matter what they say or how they act, children long to hear kind words from their parents. That's why it hurts them so much when you are mean to them either with your words or with your tone. Of course we need to be firm with our kids sometimes, but we never need to be harsh.

Harsh words do bruise the heart of a child—and eventually they break it.

MY THOUGHTS:

_____

_____

_____

FIRST-TIME DRIVER

Is it time for you to get out of the driver's seat?

A few years ago my friend Jerry's 15-year-old daughter had just gotten her restricted driver's license. And you know what that meant. Old dad had to white knuckle it from the passenger's side. Talk about nerve-wracking!! But believe it or not, Jerry said the worst part wasn't the close calls with curbs, cars and trees. It was realizing that his little girl was growing up, and that he needed to start letting go. Allowing our children to begin taking control of their own lives can feel like a bumpy ride.

But letting go is the only way they'll ever find the road to independence.

MY THOUGHTS:

MACARTHUR, THE FATHER

General Douglas MacArthur has something important to tell you.

In a 1942 speech, the military leader said, "By profession, I am a soldier, and I take great pride in that fact. But I am prouder, infinitely prouder, to be a father. A soldier destroys in order to build. The father only builds and never destroys. The one has the potentialities of death, the other embodies creation and life. It is my hope that my son, when I'm gone, will remember me not from the battle, but in the home."

Well said, General MacArthur. Well said.

MY THOUGHTS:

FAMILY MINUTES

LET IT GO

These three little words can make your marriage stronger—*let it go*.

That's right. *Let it go.* You see, too many times in marriage we focus only on what our spouse is doing wrong. It gets to be a bad habit, nit-picking them for everything. So, instead, try this. The next time your spouse does something minor—forgets to take out the trash, leaves the garage door open or doesn't pick up the milk—now you know what to do. Take a deep breath. Bite your tongue if you have to. Cut them some slack, and show them some grace.

LET IT GO!

MY THOUGHTS:

READING TIME

When's the last time you read a book to your children?

Are you having a hard time remembering? Well, you're not alone. Sixty percent of parents never read to their kids. If that's you, then it's time to turn some pages. Story time can improve your children's reading skills and can help you bond with them. Just the act of sitting side by side while you read together is a wonderful way to strengthen relationships. If your kids are older and already know how to read, let them tell you the story. Show interest. Ask questions.

Make reading together a regular part of your routine.

MY THOUGHTS:

SERVING YOUR FAMILY

Do you have the desire to help others?

After the terrorist attacks we saw rescue workers risking their lives to help those in need. The tragedy ignited a renewed spirit of service in Americans. Even though most of us couldn't help out at the attack sites, we can bring that spirit into our homes by serving our own family. It can be something as small as helping our spouse with the laundry or yard work, or praising our children when they volunteer to read a book to their younger sibling.

Let's serve those closest to us and live that spirit of service every day.

MY THOUGHTS:

MAN'S BEST FRIEND

What can you learn from man's best friend?

You can actually learn a lot of lessons from the humble dog. Here are just a few of them. Be a dependable friend. Love children. Show pleasure when treated well, and don't be afraid to express your affections. Show excitement when a family member walks in the door. Don't judge people based on how they look or the clothes they wear. And, finally, guard faithfully the interests of those who care about you.

So the next time you're with your dog, pay attention. He just might be trying to teach you a few new tricks.

MY THOUGHTS:

_____

_____

_____

FRIENDS

Do your kids know good from bad when it comes to friends?

Any police officer will tell you that your child's first cigarette will come from a friend. It will also be a friend who'll ask him or her to shoplift, go drinking or try sex. While the wrong kind of friends will weaken your child's standards, the right kind can help them stay on track. Still, your child might argue, "Don't worry, Dad. I'll be the one influencing them. They won't change me."

But a wise man said, "Bad company corrupts good character." So use your authority as a parent to teach your children how to discern good influences from bad. Remember, we are all influenced by the company we keep.

MY THOUGHTS:

_____

_____

_____

MVP

Can you name this season's most valuable player?

Go ahead and make a guess. Oh, you want to know which sport. Well, it's not a sport at all. In fact, almost everyone is eligible. You see, I'm talking about an MVP award within families. And since it's such a great honor, award it every month or even every week. Get your kids together and set the MVP criteria. There may be recognition for doing an extra chore without being asked or having a good attitude when everyone else is pouting. The point is, excellence should be noted and appreciated.

So draw up your ballots and take a vote. Who knows, Mom and Dad, maybe you'll get the prize.

MY THOUGHTS:

STRENGTH-CENTERED COMPLIMENT

All compliments are not created equal.

While getting a compliment is great, getting a strength-centered compliment is even better. Here's the difference. A general compliment sounds like this: "Honey, you look great tonight." But a strength-centered compliment takes it a step further. "Wow! That shirt really brings out the beautiful color in your eyes!"

So instead of saying this: "You're a great dad." Try this: "The way you give your kids your full attention when they're talking is so wonderful." See the difference? Try to go for the power of strength-centered compliments.

MY THOUGHTS:

_____

_____

_____

THE HEALTHY HUSBAND

Married men live longer, healthier lives than unmarried men.

A big reason is their wives tend to be more health savvy than they are. Men tend to ignore health problems, especially those that can cause them to miss work. But, guys, listen to your wives when they suggest you visit the doctor about those back pains you've been having or about that lingering cough. And try not to see her concerns as nagging.

Take your wife's advice and get health conscious for your own sake and for the sake of your family.

MY THOUGHTS:

_____

_____

_____

STRONG-WILLED CHILD

How do you handle a strong-willed child?

First, think about your own behavior. Do you speak to your child with a harsh, angry and demoralizing voice? Do you find yourself saying things like, "You're a really bad boy"? Or, "Why do you always act so stupid?" Or do you respond with a calm, firm and controlled demeanor? But, you say, "It's my child's behavior that's causing everyone grief. So why is it up to me?" Well, the greatest potential for control of your child's behavior is in his or her environment, and a huge part of that environment is you.

How you talk to and treat your child will shape their behavior.

MY THOUGHTS:

_____

_____

_____

FOCUS

If you're worried about how your children will turn out, maybe you need a two-by-four!

Dallas Cowboys' coach Jimmy Johnson huddled with his players just before the 1993 Super Bowl. He said that if you laid a two-by-four on the ground, you could walk across it with no problem. But if you put the board between two buildings ten stories high, you probably wouldn't make it since your focus would now be on how to avoid falling.

Sounds like a lesson for parents! Are you focused on your children's success or on their failure? If you focus on what they're doing right instead of on what they're doing wrong, chances are, you'll get through parenting without falling. By the way, Dallas won the game 52 to 7.

MY THOUGHTS:

_____

_____

_____

General Marriage

FAMILY MINUTES

SURRENDERED WIFE

A few years ago a book caused quite a stir.

The book is called *The Surrendered Wife*, and the author, who describes herself as a "feminist," says she has the secret to making your marriage click. But to me, the so-called "secret" is just common sense. The author says that the more wives criticize and correct their husbands, the more wimpy and resentful their husbands become. Well, that works both ways doesn't it?

Bottom line: whether it's a surrendered wife or a surrendered husband, bossiness has no place in a happy marriage.

MY THOUGHTS:

_____

_____

_____

January 18   *18*

SMART KIDS

Is there a way you can help make your kids smarter?

A scientist in early brain development was asked that question, and this was his answer: "The best evidence we have suggests that one of the best predictors of cognitive success is not buying your baby a mobile; it's not even getting them to speak French by the age of one and a half. It actually has to do with the emotional stability of the home." Wow.

So what is the bottom line? Parents who have healthy marriages will have less stress at home. And that's what helps kids' brains grow smarter.

MY THOUGHTS:

_____

_____

_____

SINGLE PARENT—REACH OUT

It's time to reach out if you're a single parent.

If the demands on you as a single parent keep you isolated from your friends and family, it's time to do something about it. I know you don't have much time. But you'll be amazed at the new energy you'll have to devote to your child if you allow yourself the renewal of friendship and kinship. Are there relatives that could baby-sit for you? Do you have neighbors you can hang out with or a friend to go to dinner with? Maybe there is a new activity at your church?

And don't worry. You're not being selfish. Whatever helps you will help your child.

MY THOUGHTS:

_____

_____

_____

SPOUSAL STRESS

Do you know how tough your spouse's job is?

A friend of mine recently helped her husband at work. He's a dentist, and she assisted him with a root canal. Later she commented on how stressful it was. Her experience gave her a better understanding of what he goes through every day. Do you know the pressures your spouse faces? Put yourself in their shoes and empathize with their challenges. Be available when they want to talk, and cut them some slack when work makes them a little edgy.

Make it your job to understand theirs.

MY THOUGHTS:

FIRST FIVE MINUTES

It all starts with "the first five minutes."

In the morning the first five minutes between a parent and child set the tone for everything to follow. They determine how a mom or dad will interact with their child that day. If you speak harsh words or act tense as the kids gather for breakfast, the relationship will end up sunny side down. And if you do start the day that way, then greet your children after school with encouraging words and a good snack. That will bring a smile to their afternoon. And at the end of the day, tuck your kids into bed with words of praise and set a positive tone for tomorrow.

MY THOUGHTS:

_____

_____

_____

General Parenting

WHAT KIND OF DAD?

What kind of relationship did you have with your dad?

Were you close? Were you afraid of him? Did you even get to spend time with him? Try to remember how it felt to be a child and what you wanted from your father. I'm asking you to do this because I want you to think about the kind of father you are to your own kids. Once you've thought about it—take action.

Be there for your children and really listen to them. Show them and tell them you love them. So one day, when they think about their father, they'll look back with a smile.

MY THOUGHTS:

FAMILY MINUTES

COOL AS A CUCUMBER

Are you cool as a cucumber or hot as a chili pepper?

If you and your child are both chili peppers, then the recipe gets even hotter when you're mixed together. Your hot temper and impatient personality will certainly evoke a defiant reaction in your impatient, quick-tempered child. And your impulsiveness may lead you to speak to your child before you think it through or to respond inconsistently. That inconsistency has long been known to cause children lots of anxiety, which often brings out defiant reactions.

So remember, one way to cool down that hot chili pepper is to mix it with a cucumber.

MY THOUGHTS:

_____

_____

_____

POWER OF GRANDPARENTS

Grandparents, your grandchildren need you.

Growing up, I was blessed with grandparents who often shared wonderful stories about my ancestors. I now realize that one of the contributions a grandparent can make is to teach their grandchildren about their family history—about the tough times the family faced and overcame and the good times it enjoyed. An old African song says, "When an old man dies, it's as if a library burns down."

Grandparents, you are the library for your grandchildren, connecting them with the pages of their past.

MY THOUGHTS:

DIVORCE CYCLE

Do you know how to break the cycle of divorce?

If you grew up in a home impacted by divorce, does that mean you're destined for a breakup too? Absolutely not. Even though studies show that children of divorce are more likely to divorce, you can break the cycle. How? Have a mindset of a lifetime commitment. Believe that you can and will work through the rough spots. Make your marriage your top priority. Work at it, and, if you need to, get help. Finally, realize the terrible toll divorce takes on children.

Do all you can to keep your marriage healthy and whole.

MY THOUGHTS:

_____

_____

_____

PARENTING VICTORIES

The thrill of victory and the agony of defeat.

Remember that slogan from the "Wide World of Sports"? Well, as a parent, I can relate. I've certainly had challenging moments in raising my three children. But when I least expect it, I get the thrill of a small but significant victory. Just the other night my daughter disobeyed me. I was waiting for, "What did I do?" But this time she said, "I know what I did was wrong, Dad. What are the consequences?" Wow! I just about passed out.

So hang tough! The thrill of victory is worth the work and the wait.

MY THOUGHTS:

IS SOMEONE AVOIDING YOU?

Is someone you care about avoiding you?

A friend of mine had a falling out with her daughter. The young woman basically cut off all contact with her mother. And in this day of answering machines and caller ID, the daughter has been able to avoid her mother's calls. So my friend is trying the old-fashioned approach. She mails her daughter a card every week. She tells her that she loves her and that she can always come home. Recently, my friend found out that her daughter is reading those cards.

Maybe one day she'll get to tell her child she loves her—face to face.

MY THOUGHTS:

_____

_____

_____

PAUL HARVEY

Who's the most listened to person on radio in America?

Let me give you a hint. He says things like, "Good day." And, "Now you know the rest of the story." Of course I'm talking about Paul Harvey. Harvey's been on the airwaves since the 1940s, and he's covered everything from the Second World War to a string of presidents. So what does he think is the most important story he's ever covered? Well, he says it was the birth of his son, Paul Junior.

Imagine that. A man who's heard by 22 million people a day and has seen it all says the thing that touched his life the most was becoming a father.

MY THOUGHTS:

_____

_____

_____

BE CAREFUL WHAT YOU ASK FOR

If you're a mom or dad, be careful what you ask for.

The late humorist Erma Bombeck wrote a column warning parents to cherish the childhood years because in the blink of an eye, they'll be gone. "Imagine," she says, "washing clothes only once a week. Having your teeth cleaned without a baby on your lap. No P.T.A. meetings. No car pools or blaring radios."

"Think about it," she says, "No more presents out of toothpicks and macaroni. No more anxious nights with a feverish child. No more sloppy oatmeal kisses. No more tooth fairy. No giggles in the dark. Only a voice crying, 'Why don't you grow up?' and the silence echoing, 'I did.'"

MY THOUGHTS:

_____

_____

_____

BEST PLACE TO CALL HOME

What if you no longer can take care of a loved one?

That realization is often difficult to accept, and you might feel that a nursing home is your only option. But there are other choices like home health and adult daycare to consider. They may be less expensive and more appropriate in your situation than the twenty-four-hour care that nursing homes provide.

If a nursing home, however, is your family's only option, there are steps you can take to make sure you choose the right one. First, make a personal inspection. Ask to see the residents' rooms, activity areas and the kitchen. Are they clean and well-maintained? Second, ask more questions. Inquire about the credentials of key caregivers. Does the facility hold a superior rating? Third, review state and federal surveys. They contain a wealth of information. Finally, ask other families and physicians about the facility.

Taking these steps can help ensure that your loved one's residence is a place they'll want to call home.

MY THOUGHTS:

_____

_____

_____

I DIDN'T KNOW WE WERE POOR

How can you be poor and not know it? I'll tell you how.

American football hero Frank Gifford says that when he was a little boy they passed around a basket at church one Sunday. The preacher said it was to help a poor family. People dropped in money and food, and the boy even threw in a dime. Well, he didn't think much more of it until the next day when he saw that basket sitting on his family's kitchen table. The poor family was his!! He says he had never thought of his home that way, and he never felt poor. He just saw a mom and dad who worked hard, loved each other and loved their children.

You see, love can make even a little seem like a lot.

MY THOUGHTS:

_____

_____

_____

Inspirational

THANK A TEACHER

When's the last time you thanked a teacher?

They help shape the future of our children and our world. But how often do we think about the huge job teachers must do? And along with a demanding job come other incredible challenges: large class sizes, reduced budgets and often unsupportive parents. So what can you do? At the very least, write your child's teacher a thank you note. Better yet, offer to decorate their classroom, donate supplies or plan a teacher appreciate luncheon. If your children are grown, you can still volunteer at a local school.

Find a special way to thank a teacher.

MY THOUGHTS:

FAMILY MINUTES

SURVIVOR

Do your kids really know what it takes to survive?

On the TV show "Survivor," people volunteer to be marooned on a remote island, and the last one standing gets a million bucks. Well, you can use the "Survivor" strategy to find out what your kids are really thinking and what they value. Ask them, "If you were stranded on a desert island and could take only five items with you, what would they be? How about if you could take only two other people? Who would you take?" What about books or food? Can you guess what your kids would answer?

Set out on an adventure to find out what your children think they need to survive. Nobody will win a million bucks, but knowing your kids are well-equipped for life is worth a whole lot more.

MY THOUGHTS:

_____

_____

_____

FAMILY TIME FAMINE

Did you know that your children may be starving and you don't even realize it?

Our country is experiencing a major famine. It's affecting thousands of children and has serious consequences. What is it? I call it the Family Time Famine. Today most kids spend more time watching TV than they spend with their parents. The Family Time Famine leaves children hungry for affection and attention. Kids spell love T-I-M-E. So do your part to stop this famine. Start in your own home with your own family.

Give your children the love and emotional food they need—your time.

MY THOUGHTS:

MORE, MORE, MORE

Is your family's motto, "I want that"?

The list of "I wants" can go on and on. For kids it's, "I want that video game. I want that scooter."

For us it's "I want that car. I want that couch."

No matter what we have, there's always more. So how do we change our perspective? Henry David Thoreau said, "We make ourselves rich by making our wants few." Ah, it's the old "being content with what you have" lesson. But to get there, we have to adjust our expectations.

Most of us already have what we need. Now it's just a matter of controlling what we "want."

MY THOUGHTS:

_____

_____

_____

DEAD-END RELATIONSHIPS

Are you single and in a dead-end relationship?

I see it a lot. Single friends stuck in a relationship going nowhere. Why do they stay? Well, people often figure that it's better to have someone than to have no one. But here's the problem with that reasoning. If you stay with the wrong person, how will you ever meet the right one? So while you're playing the dating game, set ground rules, especially if you hope to get married. Think about limiting how long you'll wait for a commitment. Don't let the power of physical attraction cloud your judgment and lure you into staying put.

And, finally, study their character. See what they're really made of.

MY THOUGHTS:

FAMILY MINUTES

THE KEY TO DISCIPLINE

What's the hardest thing about disciplining your kids?

If you're like most parents, the toughest thing is being consistent. You can read all the books in the world and have dozens of great ideas, but if you're not consistent—they won't work. I'll admit it, being consistent is tough. Sometimes it's easier to just let the kids get away with something rather than sticking to a plan and being consistent with discipline. But, hey, Mom and Dad, consistency pays off in the long run. It helps kids to know what to expect, to understand the boundaries and to respect rules instead of testing them.

So stick with it!

MY THOUGHTS:

Finances

MONEY TALK

If your kids won't listen to your financial advice, maybe they will listen to one of the world's richest men.

Billionaire Warren Buffett rarely speaks in public. So when he does, people listen. Buffett took the stage a few years ago at a conference for high school students. Want to know what advice the investment wizard gave the crowd, what moneymaking secret he shared? Of all things, Buffett zeroed in on the dangers of credit cards and said, "If you can't afford it, don't buy it." I know, you've probably told your kids the very same thing. Well, tell them again.

And now that you have Buffett behind you, this time they just might listen.

MY THOUGHTS:

FAMILY FIRST

Caution—what you're about to read might hit close to home.

If you've been spending too much time on the job and not enough time with your family, consider these comments from a study conducted a few years ago.

A 10-year-old girl says, "Your children are the most important part of your life—love them more than work."

A 12-year-old boy feels the same way. He says, "I wish you would stop working so much and spend more time with us."

An 11-year-old girl put it this way, "You don't know how much it hurts when you think your parents love their job more than you."

Could these statements apply to you? Why not ask your own children to find out.

MY THOUGHTS:

_____

_____

_____

PERFECTIONIST SPOUSE

Feel like you can't do anything right for your spouse?

It's not easy being married to someone with perfectionist tendencies. Just ask my wife! So how do you handle it? Tell the perfectionist that you do care about what's important to him or her, and show them you're doing your best whether it's keeping the house neat, the car clean or the laundry done. But also explain that when you're raising kids the house won't always look like a model home, the socks won't always be clean and the yard probably won't be perfectly manicured.

Tell them, however, that they should look on the bright side. Things will smooth out when the kids are grown. And you know what? They will probably wish things weren't so perfect after all.

MY THOUGHTS:

BOTTOMS UP

The longer your child puts off taking that first drink, the better.

Studies show that the younger you are when you start drinking, the greater your chance of becoming an alcoholic. Forty percent of kids who start drinking before age 15 (and, yes, it does happen) become alcoholics. Waiting until age 17 is not much better. Almost one-quarter of those kids will develop a drinking problem. And 1 out of 10 people who start drinking at age 21 will also have problems.

The moral to this story: protect your children by teaching them what you know about the dangers of drinking.

MY THOUGHTS:

A SINGLE VALENTINE

It's almost Valentine's Day, but if you're a single parent do you even care?

Perhaps the last thing a single parent wants to discuss on Valentine's Day is romance. So how do you share a healthy perspective on love with your children if you've been deeply wounded? While it's okay to share the hurt of your broken heart, you should also share the hope. Our kids probably already know that not every love story has a happy ending. As parents, however, we need to make sure they know that having a lasting, loving relationship is possible.

So use Valentine's Day as a conversation starter. Talk to your kids about what makes a relationship last.

MY THOUGHTS:

CHOCOLATE

Go ahead and enjoy that Valentine's Day chocolate without guilt.

Who would have guessed it? Chocolate can be good for you. At least that's what "preliminary research" shows. It says that cocoa beans contain antioxidants which might reduce the risk of heart disease.

You know what else is good for your heart? Marriage. That's right. Many studies show that being married (even if it's not always wedded bliss) can actually help you live a longer, healthier life. In one study married men with unhealthy hearts lived three years longer than unmarried men with healthy hearts.

So here's to chocolate bars and wedding vows. Happy Valentine's Day!

MY THOUGHTS:

_____

_____

_____

SPELL LOVE THIS VALENTINE'S DAY

Let love be your guide this Valentine's Day.

Want a better relationship with your spouse? Then start by studying the word LOVE. L is for listen. Pay full attention when your partner talks. Stop what you're doing and don't interrupt. O is for observe. Make getting to know their likes and dislikes a priority. V is for value. Value them for who they are. Learn to appreciate what makes them unique. And, finally, E is for encourage. Encourage them with your words and actions.

Four little letters that spell out the lessons in love.

MY THOUGHTS:

MIRACLE ON ICE

They called it "The Miracle on Ice."

The U.S. hockey team shocked the world at the 1980 Lake Placid Olympics by upsetting the Soviets four goals to three. How did they do it? Hockey watchers say the Americans won because they were willing to play as a team. There were no prima donnas, and no one was trying to hog the spotlight. That's pretty much the way a family should operate—as a team. Each member needs to put the good of the group ahead of individual desires.

When that happens, the strength of the family as a whole can lead to greater success for everyone.

MY THOUGHTS:

_____

_____

_____

SHOW LOVE

How do your kids know you love them?

To find out what they think, just ask them. That's what I did. I recently asked my 9-year-old daughter, "How do you know I love you?

She responded, "Because you tickle me."

Then I asked, "Well what if my hands were held behind my back, and I couldn't tickle you? Then how would you know I love you?"

She answered, "Because you spend time with me."

Kids realize that we spend our time on what matters most to us. So when you choose to spend your time with your children, it tells them that you love them and they really matter.

MY THOUGHTS:

_____

_____

_____

February 16

STORY TIME

"Tell me another story, Daddy!"

You know what stories my kids love to hear the most? Believe it or not, their favorite stories are of when my wife and I were children. At bedtime my 8-year-old daughter loves for me to tell her things I did when I was a child—like the time I got so homesick at camp that I wrote home every day and begged my parents to get me out of there! I think she likes these stories so much because, in a way, she gets to relate to her parents as children.

So think about your own childhood. And by sharing your memories, you'll make new ones with your own kids.

MY THOUGHTS:

BIZ TRAVEL

What's the big killer of family time?

Traveling too much on business trips really cuts into time with your family. When your job requires you to travel two to three nights a week, you're missing about 30 percent of your family's life. The consequences can be devastating. Pretty soon your spouse and children start learning to live without you. And you'll more than likely miss school plays, birthday parties and ball games. You'll also be gone for routine but important times like putting the kids to bed and eating together.

So if too much business travel is hurting your family, it may be time to stay put.

MY THOUGHTS:

WORDS KIDS HATE TO HEAR

Can you guess which two words kids hate to hear?

The words are—wait and later.

As in, "Mom, can you read me a story?"

"Wait one minute, honey."

"Dad, can you ride bikes with me?"

"Later son, half time's almost here."

And then there is, "Mom, can I ask you a quick question?"

"Wait just a second. I have one more call to make."

Well, the problem is that "wait a minute" can turn into hours, and "later" often ends up meaning never.

Of course you'll have to say "wait" and "later" sometimes. But make sure that when you do, you follow through.

MY THOUGHTS:

EATING TOGETHER PAYS OFF

If you want to make mealtimes healthier, there are only two things you have to do.

First, commit to eating together more often as a family. And, second, make sure the TV is off during mealtimes. A Baylor College of Medicine study found that when kids ate with their family, they ate more vegetables, drank less soda and ate more foods that were lower in fat. The report also says that the TV should not be invited to dinner. A lot of parents use the TV to entertain their kids during meals. The focus, however, should be on the food and the fellowship between you and your children—not on the tube.

So pull up a chair and fix a plate with the good things.

MY THOUGHTS:

_____

_____

_____

February 20

PRESIDENTS' DAY—WASHINGTON

If often takes personal sacrifice to be a great leader.

America's first president, George Washington, served his country in the War for Independence before he was elected to office. Though he led a very public life, Washington was actually a quiet man, who preferred privacy over politics. Yet, Washington sacrificed his own preferences and happiness to lead his country. He knew that a leader must at times put the needs of the people first.

If you're a parent, keep Washington in mind and be willing to put the needs of your family ahead of your own.

MY THOUGHTS:

RIGHT CHOICES

If you have a child under the age of 14, I have important news for you.

Your child will soon be driving a car on his or her own. They'll be dating and attending high school functions on their own. They will be making decisions on their own. So show them the importance of making the right choices. Show them that it's okay to be different. Show them how to stand out in the crowd and stand up for what is right, no matter what others say.

Notice I said "show them." That means you, Mom and Dad. Stand up and stand out. Your child is watching.

MY THOUGHTS:

_____

_____

_____

STEPPARENTING WITH LOVE AND STRUCTURE

It's amazing what love and structure can do.

Not too long ago a friend of mine became a stepmom when her husband's teenage daughter moved in. Before that, the girl had experienced little structure. She didn't even have to go to school. Well, my friend said school was a must—unless her stepdaughter was ill. She monitored both her internet activity and the music she listened to. And along with the structure, she showed love—a girl's night with nail painting and a slumber party for her stepdaughter's friends.

Well, it's working. That teenage girl who rarely went to school is now on the honor roll.

MY THOUGHTS:

_____

_____

_____

TIME FLIES

How many years do you really have with your kids?

You see, when puberty hits, your relationship with your kids changes, mainly because their interests change. They see things differently. Old Mom and Dad just aren't as cool as they used to be, and they want to spend more time with their friends. So do everything you can to be with your children as much as possible before that shift. Then, when it happens, keep loving, hugging and connecting with them.

Even if they don't think you're cool, they'll know you love them.

MY THOUGHTS:

JUST LIKE DAD

Would you want your daughter to marry someone like you?

The old saying goes: girls pick out husbands who are often like their dads. How does that sit with you? Our girls are watching us for an example of what to expect from their future spouse. Are you kind to your wife? Do you encourage her? What about your daughter? Do you hug her and tell her you love her? Are you there when she needs you? If you aren't, it's not too late to change. Sit down with your daughter and talk about the things you've done right—and wrong.

Show her by word and example that the man in her life should treat her with respect and love.

MY THOUGHTS:

WEEKEND RUSH

Are your family's weekends just as busy as the weekdays?

Saturdays can easily feel like Mondays. You're up early, and you rush from activity to activity—a ball game at eight, practice at ten thirty, and a birthday party at two. Whew! Where's the fun in that? Sure, you need to keep your commitments, whether they're on the weekend or not. But try to put some leisure time into your downtime. Hang out at home for a pancake breakfast. Pop some popcorn. Get the kids together and watch a movie at noon.

Enjoy some non-hectic time for a weekend that really refreshes.

MY THOUGHTS:

_____

_____

_____

FAMILY MINUTES

BOYS AND BOOKS

Boys and books can be a great mix.

After your son has learned to read, you can take steps to ensure that he enjoys reading. An article in the *Orlando Sun-Sentinel* gives some great ideas to motivate boys to read. First, it's important to know that boys like non-fiction books—books about sports and adventure. Next, you can encourage your son by giving books as presents. When you give him a soccer ball, for instance, include a book on the sport. And, finally, make reading a regular part of your household activities. Let your son see you read.

Boys and books are a winning combination.

MY THOUGHTS:

_____

_____

_____

Fatherhood

DAD FOR HIRE

Are your children really your priority?

A man came home from work tired and irritable. Before he could catch his breath, his little boy bombarded him with questions. "Daddy, how much money do you make an hour?"

"I don't have time for this," the man growled.

The boy persisted, "How much, Daddy?"

The man snapped, "Twenty dollars!"

"Well, Daddy, can I have ten dollars?"

"Son, I told you, I'm busy."

"Okay, Daddy."

Later the dad went to the boy's room to apologize. "Sorry, Son, here's the ten dollars."

The boy smiled and pulled out ten more crumpled bills from under his pillow. "Thank you, Daddy. Now I have enough money to buy one hour of your time. So, Daddy, how about now?"

MY THOUGHTS:

_____

_____

_____

FAMILY MINUTES

TEACHING COMPASSION

Are you teaching your kids to be compassionate?

Think back to your school days. Remember the child who was different? Maybe he wore old clothes, had a disability or didn't look like everyone else. Well, these children are still around. That's why it's important that we teach our children to be compassionate, to be kind to children who are different instead of making things harder for them. Explain to your kids why showing compassion toward others is the right thing to do.

Let them know you expect it. And show them how to give it by being compassionate yourself.

MY THOUGHTS:

TALKING TIPS

Are your kids in the one-word-answer stage?

It can start when they're as young as 5 years old and sounds like this: "What did you do today?"

"Nothing."

"How did your test go?"

"Okay."

"Are you hungry?"

"Yes."

Riveting stuff, huh? Well, if you want to get better answers, ask better questions—questions that will evoke more than a one-word response. "What was the best part of school today?" "If you could cook, what would you make for dinner tonight?" And, "How do you feel about your math test?"

Those are the kinds of questions that will take you beyond yes and no and will lead to better communication and a deeper relationship with your kids.

MY THOUGHTS:

_____

_____

_____

TO THE RESCUE

Men, do you want to be your wife's hero?

Awhile ago my wife told me about a challenging situation she was in. I immediately swooped in for the rescue and gave her the solution, "Do A, B and C. There, the problem is solved." That's what I thought. But the look in her eyes told me it wasn't. You see, my wife wanted to talk things through. She needed me to listen and show compassion, not jump in and fix the problem.

So the next time your wife starts talking about a challenge in her life, leave your Superman cape in the closet and be a hero by listening.

MY THOUGHTS:

_____

_____

_____

WHO ARE YOU?

One day you wake up and there's a stranger next to you!

I don't have to tell you that time flies. One day our kids are crawling. The next day they're driving off to college. And in between it seems like all we have time for is meeting the needs of our children. But what about that other person, you know, your husband or wife? When your kids leave the nest will you be staring at a stranger? It can happen. So every week, have a date with your spouse.

If you make sure to spend time alone with your husband or wife now, you will still have your best friend around when those empty nest days arrive. And for all parents, that day will come!

MY THOUGHTS:

March 4

VALUABLES

What do you hold dearest to your heart?

Not too long ago three grown children had to go through their father's belongings after he died. Their dad had been a successful businessman and left behind lots of files and paperwork. When the children were just about finished cleaning things out they found a key to a safe deposit box where they expected to find more business documents. But when they opened it, tears filled their eyes. The box was overflowing with construction paper hearts, crayon drawings and cards they had made for their father while growing up. These were his most valuable papers.

So what's dearest to your heart?

MY THOUGHTS:

_____

_____

_____

TO SNOOP OR NOT TO SNOOP

Have you faced the snooping dilemma yet with your children?

It usually hits around adolescence—the secret phone calls, notes from friends at school, a carefully hidden journal. So do you snoop? Experts say no...and yes. If you're confident your child is on the straight and narrow, don't snoop. That's just being nosy. But if you suspect your child is in danger, using drugs, or having sex, then do whatever it takes to keep your child safe. Actor Carol O'Connor's son killed himself after a long battle with drugs. After his son's death, O'Connor said he regretted not stepping in sooner.

Mom and Dad, you are your child's protector.

MY THOUGHTS:

_____

_____

_____

Parenting Teens

SIGNS OF A LOVING FAMILY

Can you name the five signs of a loving family?

In his book *The Five Signs of a Loving Family*, Dr. Gary Chapman finds there are five elements that create healthy family dynamics. Chapman says the five vital signs found in any loving family are service towards one another, intimacy in marriage, parents who train their children, children who honor their parents and fathers who are loving leaders.

To find out exactly what those signs are and how to instill them in your home, visit FamilyMinute.net.

MY THOUGHTS:

PARENTAL HUMBLING

Do you owe your children an apology?

Do you have what it takes to tell your children you were wrong? Maybe you lost your temper and yelled at them for no reason. Maybe you punished them for something when they were innocent. Or, maybe you did something yourself you've told them not to do. In all of these cases, you need to ask your children for forgiveness. Don't worry. Humbling yourself before your children won't make you seem weak. Instead, it will show them just how strong you are, that you are ready to take responsibility for your mistakes.

A parent who is willing to admit that they are wrong will give their kids the courage to face their own mistakes.

MY THOUGHTS:

_____

_____

_____

HOUSE RULES

Do your kids have clear guidelines on what you expect in your home?

In our home, the house rules are posted in plain view. Rule one—we expect the kids to do what we say the first time we ask without complaining or arguing. If they don't, there are extra work assignments. Rule two—all chores must be completed each week. If they go undone the kids lose their allowance. And, finally, rule three—the children are not allowed to say mean things or hit each other. They get three chances. If they strike out, no friends over that weekend.

Spell out what you expect so your kids will know the rules of the house.

MY THOUGHTS:

_____

_____

_____

GOOD ENOUGH MARRIAGES

If your marriage is just "good enough," don't give up hope.

Research has found that things usually will get better. In fact, the study found that most of the couples with low marriage satisfaction who managed to stay married were actually very happy five years later. The study's author says, "Permanent marital unhappiness is surprisingly rare." It seems that most marriages simply go through cycles—ups and downs of happiness.

So if you stay committed and work through your problems, you can have a happy marriage that's worth fighting for.

MY THOUGHTS:

_____

_____

_____

KIDS NEED MORE SLEEP

Is your child sleep-deprived?

Sleep expert Dr. James B. Maas of Cornell University says that most children do not get the nine hours they need. And when they don't, they're more irritable, forgetful and accident-prone. To learn and function at their best, kids need nine hours. Big kids need even more. Adolescents through college age need nine hours and fifteen minutes of sleep a night.

So even if you're doing everything else right for your kids, you're setting them up for some very long days if you're not making sure they're getting enough Z's.

MY THOUGHTS:

BALANCE

Are you good at keeping your balance?

Life is a struggle for balance. Recently, I lost mine. There was just too much going on—work, travel, school, open house, ballet practice, baseball practice and on and on. The result? My wife and I were tense with each other and short with the kids. We got too busy and lost our balance. To get your balance back, take control of your family's schedule. If you don't, it will run you. Avoid setting yourself up for a frantic pace.

So to keep your life in balance, keep your schedule under control.

MY THOUGHTS:

March 12

FOULING OUT

Are you fouling out with your kids?

In his book *Leading with the Heart*, Duke basketball coach Mike Krzyzewski tells his players not to worry about the play they just messed up. In his words, "Your fifth shot is your first shot." Well, maybe you recently missed a "shot" with one of your kids. You didn't make the school play. You wrongly accused him. Or maybe you kept your eyes glued to the TV instead of listening to her. If so, don't dwell on it. Instead, go to your child and say, "I was wrong. Please forgive me."

Then, concentrate on making your next shot nothing but net.

MY THOUGHTS:

_____

_____

_____

Family Time

TAKE A BREAK

Take a break with your family.

It's that time of year. Can you feel it? It's spring break. Many will see this as just a week away from school or maybe a week away from work. But you can use this as an opportunity to do something out of the ordinary with your family. Instead of another attraction, event or theme park, take a break from it all by going camping, hiking or fishing. They're inexpensive outings and fun ways to refresh, rejuvenate and really connect as a family.

So during this spring break, take a break from all your usual activities and come together as a family.

MY THOUGHTS:

March 14

FAMILY MINUTES

I DON'T KNOW

Are you brave enough to say "I don't know" to your kids?

As parents, we're supposed to be the ones in control. So when our children ask us a question and we don't have the answer, we might be afraid to say "I don't know." However, when we admit to our kids that we don't know everything we're teaching them a couple of lessons. First, we're showing honesty. Our integrity is more important than our ego. We're also showing them that life is a learning process, and that it's okay not to know everything.

So try saying "I don't know," and then set out to find the answers together.

MY THOUGHTS:

LOVE LANGUAGE

If you feel like you can't do anything right for your spouse, maybe you're doing the wrong things.

One day I did a load of laundry for my wife. I then expected cheers and accolades from her. Although she told me she appreciated what I did, it was no big deal to her. And it was no big deal since I was not speaking her "love language." Dr. Gary Chapman says a love language is how someone wants to be shown love because it satisfies a deep-seated need.

According to Dr. Chapman, most people prefer one of five love languages when receiving expressions of love. Do you know which one is your spouse's? For example, if your husband always seems to shine when you say "I appreciate you," he probably prefers the love language of affirmation. Affirming him means to encourage and empathize with him. Does your wife feel really special when you take her on a romantic date? Then show her love through quality time. Receiving gifts is the love language for some, while others prefer to receive love through acts of service. To them a repaired washing machine or cleaned house will have more impact than a box of candy. Finally, if physical touch is your spouse's love language, give him or her a nice back rub.

Learn your spouse's love language so you can speak in a language he or she can really understand.

MY THOUGHTS:

LESSONS FROM HOUSE OF HOPE

What do teenagers need?

I talked with a 16-year-old named Shannon who lives at House of Hope, a residential treatment facility in Orlando, Florida. She grew up with all of the material comforts, but her dad was always working and her mom didn't set boundaries or discipline her. In middle school Shannon turned to drugs and sex. She says all parents can learn from House of Hope. It is a place where kids get unconditional love and structure through daily chores, schoolwork that is monitored and devotions. "Now," Shannon says, "I feel like a new person."

So what do teenagers need? Love and structure.

MY THOUGHTS:

_____

_____

_____

NCAA FINAL FOUR

Anything can happen during basketball's March Madness.

The history of the NCCA basketball tournament is full of surprises; a time when the underdog can pull off an upset. What a good reminder of what can happen to each one of us in life.

So if you're feeling like an underdog—discouraged in your marriage, frustrated with your in-laws, shut out by your teenager or overwhelmed in your responsibilities as a parent—cheer up and hang in there. Your own personal victory might be just around the corner.

Remember, just like the surprises in March Madness, there may be a good surprise awaiting you.

MY THOUGHTS:

_____

_____

_____

March 18

SPRINGTIME FUN

On your mark, get set, garden!

It's almost the first day of spring and planting a garden with your children can be a great springtime activity. If you have a yard, plant vegetables or giant sunflowers. If you have limited space, plant flowers by a window or in a window box. All you'll need are seed packets and soil. For a few dollars you'll have a project that you and your kids can enjoy for months. Give your children watering responsibility or weeding duty.

Then enjoy your harvest of vegetables, flowers and fond memories.

MY THOUGHTS:

_____

_____

_____

SPRING-FRESH START

Do your relationships need some spring cleaning?

Maybe you feel like you've blown it again. You didn't show up, you lost your temper, or you spoke down to your husband, your wife, your teenager or your co-worker. Well, to set things right, start with an apology. Say that you were wrong without making excuses. Then ask for forgiveness and tell them you want to do better. Finally, make sure your actions match your words.

Before you know it, you'll be on your way to a fresh start.

MY THOUGHTS:

March 20

SINGLE PARENT'S DAY

Did you know that there is a Single Parent's Day?

If you know a single parent, you may not realize the unending struggles they face. Maintaining a house and a career, and chauffeuring the kids to little league are hard enough when there are two parents sharing the work. But single parents do all this alone. If only they had some relief in sight. Well, you and I can give them that relief. Let's treat their family to dinner or baby-sit so they can have time to themselves. Fix their car or mow their lawn.

Not only will your help be appreciated, but it will let them know somebody cares.

MY THOUGHTS:

_____

_____

_____

YOUR LIFE STORY

Ever thought about writing your life story?

You might be thinking, "Who, me? What's so interesting about my life?" But everyone has a story to tell. And because it's your children's and grandchildren's history too, they would love to learn about your life. So set aside some time. It might take just a weekend or an hour a day until you get the job done. Start by listing the big events in your life—both happy and sad. Go through old pictures and scrapbooks to help jog your memory. Those basics will get you started. And you can visit FamilyMinute.net for more detailed help.

Start writing a history today that may last for generations.

MY THOUGHTS:

DADS AND BODY IMAGE

Dads, don't make weight an issue with your daughter.

You might think you're just being helpful when you say, "Do you really need that donut?" Or maybe you're just trying to be funny when you grab your daughter's waist and say, "Getting a little chubby, huh?"

Well, a study says that comments like those can actually set your daughter up for food and weight problems. The report found that dads who were concerned about their daughter's weight caused the girls to have a poor body image—even if they weren't heavy.

Dads, how you view your daughter carries a lot of "weight."

MY THOUGHTS:

MARRIAGE COUPONS

Want to put some fun into your marriage?

Then have I got something for you—free marriage coupons. Get them at our website, FamilyMinute.net. Give them to your spouse for whatever you want, whenever you want. How about one for a massage, a day without nagging, or mom or dad's night out? In the household chore department we have ones for doing the dishes, washing the car or making the bed. There's even one for a compliment. Just redeem it with your spouse and get a compliment back.

There are plenty more coupons. So check them out!

MY THOUGHTS:

MONEY PIT

Are your finances in the money pit?

If that's where you are, take a deep breath. Look at what got you into trouble in the first place. If it was a medical emergency or another life-or-death situation, that's one thing. But if the problem is credit card debt, you can start getting back on track today. First, start paying cash. If you can't afford it, don't buy it—period. That should stop things from getting worse. Next, go to a recommended credit counselor and let them help you set up a payment plan and a budget.

Finally, enjoy the peace that comes from taking the first steps to a debt-free life.

MY THOUGHTS:

_____

_____

_____

SPRING RUT

Are you feeling down because you're stuck in a rut?

Getting out of a rut can be as simple as getting a new haircut or as involved as going back to school. But both require you to take the first step. Call your hairdresser. Apply for college. Begin a workout routine. Sign up for music lessons, or write that book you've been thinking about.

Spring is a great time for new beginnings. So take that first step today. Get up, get going and get out of your rut.

MY THOUGHTS:

LAUGH IT OFF

How many times a day do you laugh?

Think about it—seriously. I realize some people are more jovial than others. But you're not off the hook just because you're naturally on the somber side. You see, laughing is good for you. An old proverb says, "A cheerful heart is good medicine." And science has proven it again and again. So if you're not a fun-loving kind of person, here is some home-work for you: read the comics every day. Get with a friend who makes you laugh. Watch "Three Stooges" reruns. Have your kids tickle you.

Do whatever it takes to put a smile on your face and a chuckle in your day.

MY THOUGHTS:

_____

_____

_____

WHAT IS MOST IMPORTANT?

What's most important to you?

In the movie *Beethoven*, the husband is concerned about his struggling business while the wife is concerned about their kids and their dog, Beethoven.

The husband says to the wife, "My dream is going down the tubes and all you can talk about is the dog."

The wife responds, "Our family is going down the tubes and all you can talk about is a dream."

Obviously, the husband is focused on business; the wife is focused on relationships. What's more important? Sure is something to think about.

MY THOUGHTS:

_____

_____

_____

ROOT OF THE PROBLEM

To solve marriage problems you must get to the root.

There's a large vine that wraps around a big oak tree in my backyard. If I don't cut it down, it will eventually kill the oak. But if I get to the vine's root, the problem will be solved. In marriage there is also a destructive vine—impatience, unkind words and lack of self-control. They can eventually choke the life out of our relationship. And the root cause of these problems is selfishness. Doing what's best for us, whether it hurts the other person or not.

So root out selfishness and help your marriage grow stronger.

MY THOUGHTS:

_____

_____

_____

BOY OH BOY

Who does divorce affect the most—boys or girls?

According to one study, divorce has a more negative impact on boys. A writer in *USA Today* says that even the best post-divorce circumstances cannot compensate for the sadness boys experience when their fathers leave home. So are boys of divorce destined for struggle? No. The study also says that if dads stay involved, their sons will have less depression and be less likely to have behavioral problems.

The bottom line—boys need their dads. So whether you live with your children or not, don't forget that being a part of your son's life can make all the difference.

MY THOUGHTS:

TOO MUCH TV

If your kids are always glued to the tube, I've got just the ticket.

Most of the parents I talk to agree: kids watch too much TV. One researcher estimates that in the average child's lifetime, he or she will spend more hours watching TV than sleeping. Believe it or not there is an easy way to manage TV time in your house. It's called "TV Tickets." Simply cut some paper into movie-size ticket stubs and make each ticket worth an hour. Budget your children's viewing time by giving them tickets. Maybe they earn them, maybe they're a gift.

Either way, your kids will learn to use their time wisely and see that there is life beyond the tube.

MY THOUGHTS:

_____

_____

_____

WRONG CHOICE

"Daddy, can you stay with me for a while?"

That's what my 9-year-old daughter asked me one night as I tucked her into bed. So what did I say? "I can't right now, but I'll be back in twenty minutes." Well, I'm embarrassed to admit I couldn't stay because I wanted to watch the last few minutes of a TV show. Can you believe it?! Trading a once-in-a-lifetime opportunity with my little girl to watch a crummy show!

So the next morning I told her what I had done and asked her to forgive me. Now I hope and pray that I never make the same mistake again.

MY THOUGHTS:

POWER OF FLOWERS

Dads, do you want your relationship with your daughter to bloom?

The floral industry may have the answer: research shows that most women love to get flowers. So now that you have that "scientific" data, make a point to send flowers to your daughter. That's right. Have flowers delivered to her whether she lives at home, at college or is even married and in another town. And it doesn't have to be her birthday or a holiday. Just send along a card and tell her you love her. Believe me, it will make her day.

So call a florist today, and watch the power of flowers come to life.

MY THOUGHTS:

MOVIES AND SMOKING

Can R-rated movies lead your children to dangerous habits?

A study out of Dartmouth College says they can. It found that children whose parents allow them to watch R-rated movies are three times more likely to smoke and drink than kids who are not allowed to see R-rated movies. The researchers said parents underestimate the impact movies have on kids. They also encourage parents to monitor the movies their kids watch at home.

So if you want to help your children avoid smoking and drinking, make R-rated movies off limits.

MY THOUGHTS:

_____

_____

_____

THE HOBBIT

One great writer owes his success to his children.

J.R.R. Tolkien wrote *The Hobbit.* Over the years the book has sold 35 million copies. The characters that run through *The Hobbit* came to life in stories Tolkien told his own children. You see, although Tolkien had a gift for writing, he never used it until his children inspired him to. And they were able to inspire him and bring out his talents because he spent time with them.

While the love we have for our children may make us use our talents more wisely, to really love them and get to know them, we must spend time with them. For time spent together is the source of inspiration.

MY THOUGHTS:

BUSINESS TRAVELERS

Is business travel coming between you and your kids?

If you have to be away from your family, make an effort to stay in touch. Talk to your children every day. Ask them about their schoolwork. Find out what activities or sporting events they have. And before you go out of town, leave behind a little gift or a note for each day you'll be gone. When you get home make your reunion special. Hug them and tell them you love them and missed them. Give them your undivided attention and make the most of your time together.

Instead of causing division, time away from home can provide opportunities which may in the end draw your kids closer to you.

MY THOUGHTS:

April 5

DEFIANT CHILD

Do you have a defiant child?

In their book *Your Defiant Child*, authors Russell Barkley and Christine Benton say there are three things you should do. First, know what's important to you. Make a list of your priorities for change in your child. Improved school performance? A decrease in aggressiveness toward others? Obeying mom and dad? Then focus on the most important one first.

Second, act instead of reacting to your defiant child. I know it's tough to do, but you are not at their mercy. How you interact with him in any individual encounter is your choice. If you find it difficult to try to reason with your defiant child, you're not alone. The more you talk the deeper he digs in his heels. So what's a parent to do? Well, defiant children respond much more quickly to an adult acting, not yakking. So keep your words short and your action swift.

Finally, the best way to take the initiative toward change is to have a plan for how you will act in the future. How your child acts will follow. Be calm and firm, not hot and harsh in your words, your tone of voice or your actions.

Remember, if your child is defiant you need to act so you won't end up reacting and then regretting.

MY THOUGHTS:

STRESS FACTOR

Does your family need help handling stress?

Maybe this sounds familiar. "Mom, I can't find my shoes!" "Dad, if we don't leave now we're going to be late!" Can't you just feel the tension? Well, a study found two things that can help families survive stress: commitment and appreciation. Commitment lets family members know that each person is there for the other, no matter what. Appreciation is a respect builder—saying thank you and acknowledging contributions and sacrifices made for the good of the family.

So add these two traits to your home and give stress the slip.

MY THOUGHTS:

OLDER AND WISER

It turns out the elderly possess a great weapon against stress.

A study by the University of Florida and Wayne State University, published in the *Journal of Holistic Nursing*, found that 96 percent of older adults use prayer to cope with stress. The average age of the seniors was 74 years old. Researchers discovered that the ones who prayed used more positive ways of handling the ups and downs of life than those who did not pray. The conclusion: scientists say that prayer may help seniors live healthier and less stressful lives.

And if it works for seniors, maybe we all should give it a try.

MY THOUGHTS:

LET THEM EARN IT

Can your kids have whatever they want?

Most children will want something extra at some point, a new bike when their old one is fine, the latest doll or the hottest video game. Well, the next time your child asks for something like this, tell them of course they can have it—if they earn it. Then, help them work and save for it. Give them extra chores like raking the leaves or washing the car. Keep track of their progress with a free goal chart from our website, FamilyMinute.net.

In the end, they'll have what they want, plus the experience and satisfaction of working hard to get it.

MY THOUGHTS:

FAMILY MINUTES

ENGAGEMENT ADVICE

Will your children turn to you when they need advice?

A mother I know threw an engagement party for her daughter. Along with the festivities and celebration, she talked to her child about the seriousness of the marriage commitment. She said her daughter listened to her because she, in a way, had earned the right to be heard. Over the years she'd been there for her daughter, even when it was a little thing, and had laid a foundation on which a relationship was built with time and love.

So if you want your children to listen to your advice at the big moments, be there for the little ones along the way.

MY THOUGHTS:

PARENTS DO MATTER

Can a good marriage help keep your kids out of trouble?

Do you think your kids even notice if your marriage is good or not? Do you think they care? Well, in one study more than 70 percent of the teenagers interviewed said that moms and dads with strong marriages are less likely to have children who are violent and commit crimes. Now I'm going to tell you something: those kids are onto something. And researchers at Columbia University came to the same conclusion. In their words, the erosion of family life is a primary cause of teen violence.

So if you needed another reason to work on your marriage, there it is.

MY THOUGHTS:

GOLF GAME

Want to help your kids excel in sports and life?

Tiger Woods began swinging a golf club at the age of one. When he was 3 years old he shot a legitimate 48 on nine holes, something I only dream about. And at age 24 he set a record at the U.S. Open with an astounding winning margin of 15 strokes. How does he do it? Besides his incredible talent, what makes Tiger tick? Well, Tiger himself credits unlimited love from his parents for giving him the confidence to succeed.

So if you want your children to find success, give them the love that can help make them champions in life.

MY THOUGHTS:

MARATHON

Are you prepared to hit the wall in the parenting marathon?

A friend of mine once ran the Marine Corps Marathon in Washington, DC. He said that at mile twenty he hit the wall. That's the runner's way of saying, "I just don't think I have it in me to keep going." Parenting can feel that way. Physically and mentally you're exhausted. You want to throw up your hands and say, "I quit." But my runner friend pushed through the wall and finished his marathon. He said the sense of accomplishment made it all worth it.

So hang in there when you hit the wall, and imagine how great you'll feel when your kids cross the finish line into adulthood.

MY THOUGHTS:

FAMILY MINUTES

BIGGER AND BIGGER

America's kids are getting bigger and bigger.

A few years ago a government report said the percentage of overweight kids had doubled since 1980. Wow! That's not good. Extra weight in the early years can turn into a life-long weight problem, which often raises serious health risks. So what can you do if your children fall into this category? Get them moving. Whether it's soccer, swimming or a game of kickball at home, activity takes off the pounds. After that, make sure your kids have healthy snacking options that are easy to get to and taste good.

Work fitness and careful snacking into your family's lifestyle to keep your kids healthy.

MY THOUGHTS:

LIFELINE

Did you ever watch the hit TV show "Who Wants to Be a Millionaire"?

There is something on that show that may help you in life. Now if you win a million dollars that will obviously help. But there's a lesson in all the trivia and suspense. Contestants get to use lifelines to help them answer the questions. Lifelines are a last resort, something to hold onto when the chips are down. One lifeline allows you to phone a friend for help. Who are your lifelines? Make a list. Then, the next time you're in a bind or feel alone, instead of worrying or eating a gallon of ice cream, call one of your lifelines.

Who knows, they might just have the million-dollar answer to your problem.

MY THOUGHTS:

FAMILY MINUTES

APRIL SHOWERS

You know the saying, April showers bring May flowers.

Try to remember that when you come across the rough patches in your marriage. When you do encounter those tough times, your first instinct might be to give up, especially when the trials are ongoing. But good can come out of those challenging times if you make up your mind to stick it out, work through your problems and recommit to your marriage.

Adversity can be the showers that help your relationship bloom into an even greater love.

MY THOUGHTS:

_____

_____

_____

ALL EARS

Men, are you only half listening when someone is talking to you, especially your wife?

Well, science has proven that most men really aren't good listeners. An Indiana University researcher found that men listen with only half their brains while women use both sides. So, men, is it hopeless? Absolutely not! Here are some simple ways you can improve your listening skills. First, give your wife your full attention. Put down the remote, stop reading the paper and make eye contact. Next, concentrate on what's being said instead of thinking about your response. And, finally, don't interrupt.

Are you listening? What your wife has to say may be more important than you think.

MY THOUGHTS:

_____

_____

_____

WORDS OF A TEEN KILLER

A teenage killer sends a chilling message.

Do you think the movies and music your children watch and listen to don't affect them? Well, that's what Jamie Ross thought—until he walked into his Tennessee high school and shot a student and teacher. Now he says, "The whole time it affected me. It helped shape the way I thought. All those songs and movies make killing look cool." While Jamie acknowledges that not all kids who listen to and watch violent images will turn to murder, still the damage is being done.

"It has already influenced you," he says, "and you just don't realize it."

MY THOUGHTS:

_____

_____

_____

GOOD FATHER

How do you know you're being a good father?

I thought about that one day and came up with some things that show me I'm at least making some progress. Like when my son or daughter comes running to me when they get hurt. When my calendar is full of things to do with my children. When I calmly and gently discipline without yelling or screaming. When I tuck my children into bed and tell them "I love you" and pray with them. When I make breakfast for them and drive them to school. These are just some of the things that let me know I'm actually getting it right.

What about you?

MY THOUGHTS:

_____

_____

_____

April 19

FAMILY MINUTES

TRUSTING TEENS

So your teenager says you don't trust him.

Your response might be something like, "No, it's not that we don't trust you being out so late, it's just that…" Then you run out of words and go on the defensive. If you're a parent in that situation, remind your children that trust is something that is earned with age and action. Explain to your kids that they will be able to make more decisions as they get older. And, that each time they show through their actions that they can handle privileges in a trustworthy manner, they will be given more latitude.

Don't go on the defensive. Instead, take the offensive approach by working with your teen on the issue of trust.

MY THOUGHTS:

IMPORTANT MARITAL ASSET

What is one of your most important marital assets?

It's a positive attitude! Life is 10 percent what happens to you and 90 percent how you react to it. So how can you change a lousy attitude into a positive one? First, look for the positive. Abraham Lincoln said, "If you look for the bad in mankind expecting to find it, you surely will." Second, refuse to be a victim. Self-pity is a luxury no marriage can afford. Third, give up grudges. They only clog the veins of a positive attitude.

Changing an attitude won't occur overnight so be patient and don't give up.

MY THOUGHTS:

WHAT TEENS NEED

What do teenagers need most?

Self-esteem is at the top of the list of what teens need. So what do you do if your teenager has low self-esteem? Well, find something they're good at or interested in and really support them. Help them find ways to grow and succeed in that area. If it's sports, practice with them or sign them up for a clinic. If it's music, make sure they have the tools to succeed. Whatever it is, make sure you do everything possible for them to achieve.

And as their successes increase, so will their self-esteem.

MY THOUGHTS:

A CHILD'S VOCABULARY

If you want your child to have a big vocabulary, talk to her.

Studies show that the more you talk to your child when they're a baby and toddler, the more words they will have in their vocabulary. The key here is direct communication—person to person, parent to child. Just listening to conversations doesn't have the same effect. And researchers say watching television has little positive impact on increasing a child's vocabulary.

So spend as much time as you can with your baby giving her your full attention and lots of loving words.

MY THOUGHTS:

MONEY IN THE JAR

Are your kids always asking you for money?

Teaching children how to use money wisely can be difficult. At my house we're using a very visual, hands-on way. Here's how it works. We've given each child three mason jars. When they get their allowance, they divide the money between the jars. One jar is for spending, one is for church and the final jar is for savings. We want our kids to know that money isn't just for buying things for themselves but should also be used to help others.

So give it a try. Help your children learn the fun of spending, the reward of saving, and the joy of giving.

MY THOUGHTS:

FATHER TEDDY

Teddy Roosevelt was many things, but what mattered most to him was being a father.

At the outbreak of the Spanish-American War, Roosevelt was assembling his Rough Riders in Tampa and had time to write just one letter. He sent a tender note to his children. It began, "Blessed Bunnies." Roosevelt was obviously a busy man—president, explorer, author, soldier. Still, he always made time to relate to each of his children one-on-one.

Now most of us will never be president or see our face on Mount Rushmore. We can, however, follow in Roosevelt's footsteps by being a loving and responsible dad.

MY THOUGHTS:

FAMILY MINUTES

THE GREAT OUTDOORS

Have your kids put away Nintendo and reintroduce them to the great outdoors.

With all of our modern games and conveniences, we forget to appreciate the beauty of a sunrise or to enjoy watching a rainfall. Slow down and show your children how to smell the roses. But don't just give them a canned "I'm thankful for the sun and the rain" speech. Instead, encourage your kids to discover nature for themselves. Let them run in the rain and, yes, play in the dirt. Maybe even send them on a backyard scavenger hunt to collect flowers, leaves and bugs.

You can even get out there with them and together experience the great adventures in the great outdoors.

MY THOUGHTS:

HARRY'S POWER

Harry Potter did the unimaginable.

In case you haven't heard, the *Harry Potter* book series accomplished some pretty amazing things. The series broke sales' records left and right. But even more unbelievable is that kids put down their TV remotes and video games to pick up *Potter*. That's right. They read by choice. So, parents, let's take advantage of our kids' interest in reading these books. Introduce them to great books like *Treasure Island*, *Little Women* or *The Lion, the Witch, and the Wardrobe*.

Harry Potter opened the door. Now it's up to us to go through it.

MY THOUGHTS:

CORRECTION LIMIT

How often do you correct your spouse?

Do you tell him he's not putting on the baby's diaper right? Do you tell her she's holding the map the wrong way? Do you scowl at him when he drinks out of the milk jug? Well, even when you say it nicely, correction is really hard to take. So try this: limit your correcting to once a week. If you correct your spouse all the time, they'll start feeling like they can't do anything right. And besides, who wants to be around a person who makes someone feel bad?

So let the little things go and save your correcting for what really matters.

MY THOUGHTS:

_____

_____

_____

ATTITUDE OF GRATITUDE

Do your children have an attitude of gratitude?

Raising a grateful child has never been more challenging. Our kids are bombarded constantly by ads that create expectations that their every wish should be fulfilled. The message is you need more, so buy more. And if they do get everything they want, they take it for granted. A grateful person is shaped to appreciate not just acquire. Take every opportunity to show your kids what it means to appreciate what they do have. Thank Mom for a good meal. Thank the mailman for faithfully delivering the mail. And thank the little league coach for giving his time.

An attitude of gratitude—it's a gift they'll learn to appreciate.

MY THOUGHTS:

FAMILY MINUTES

A HOT TIP

What's a stock market investor to do in a market where first it's up and then it's down?

Every good investor has vision, patience and insight. An old Chinese proverb offers this lesson. If your vision is for a year, plant wheat. If your vision is for ten years, plant trees. But if your vision is for a lifetime, plant people. Things like stocks come and go, but people will carry your values and beliefs through generations. Investing in people is the ultimate long-term view, the mutual fund of a lifetime.

So make your moves in the market, but take time to invest in the people around you.

MY THOUGHTS:

Character

THANKFULNESS

Are you teaching your children how to be thankful?

Being thankful is more than just saying "thank you." It's an attitude. It's being aware of blessings instead of taking things for granted. One way to teach children to be thankful is to have them do thank you notes for gifts. Even if they can't write yet, they can color a picture. Taking the time to show thanks helps them connect gratitude with getting.

You can also encourage gratitude by having them pray. Little children who give thanks for the small things like flowers, friends and trees will learn to live a life filled with gratitude.

MY THOUGHTS:

May 1

WORDS THAT WOUND

What do you do when you've lost control and said something that wounded your child?

The answer is to repair the damage as soon as possible. In his book *Bringing Up Boys*, Dr. James Dobson says that wounding a child with words is like taking a divot out of the turf with a golf club. The quicker you get the grass back in place, the faster its roots will reconnect. But the longer the divot bakes in the sun, the smaller its chances are for recovery.

In the same way, when you've hurt someone, you can replace the emotional divot by promptly seeking forgiveness and reconciliation. If you do, it won't be long before your relationship will grow back even stronger.

MY THOUGHTS:

_____

_____

_____

HURRICANE SEASON

Will your marriage survive the stormy weather ahead?

After Hurricane Andrew devastated South Florida in 1992, a man whose house was the only one still standing in his neighborhood said, "It hit us alright, but I built my house according to building code. I guess nobody else around here did." You see, the code requires that anything built to last must follow certain rules. That's a good lesson for marriage. We know storms will hit—arguments, heartbreak, disappointments. But a lasting marriage has its own building code. It is built on a foundation of love with materials like honor, trust and respect.

If built properly, with the right stuff, your marriage will keep standing no matter how hard the wind blows.

MY THOUGHTS:

_____

_____

_____

PREMARITAL QUESTIONS

Do you know what to ask before you say "I do"?

Before you take your vows you might want to step back and ask your true love a few questions. Are they open to moving or would they rather stay in the same town? How many kids do they want? Would they consider adoption? How frequently do they want to get together with your family? Do they plan on attending religious services? How often? Where do they want to spend the holidays?

These kinds of questions get to the heart of day-to-day married life. For more premarital questions, go to FamilyMinute.net.

MY THOUGHTS:

General Parenting

DREAM ON!

In an age of instant everything, it's nice to hear about a slow starter for a change.

Have your kids ever given up on a dream because it was taking too long? Tell them about Jim Morris. For years he dreamed of pitching in the major leagues. And although he was drafted by Milwaukee in 1983, he never made it to the majors. So he hung up his spikes to coach in high school.

Then, on a dare sixteen years later, he won a tryout. This time he pitched his way onto the mound with the Tampa Bay Devil Rays. He made his major league debut in 1999 at the age of 35 years old!

With so much emphasis today on instant success, let's teach our kids that some dreams just take time.

MY THOUGHTS:

_____
_____
_____

FAMILY MINUTES

HANDS-ON PARENTING

Want to keep your kids off drugs?

A study by the National Center on Addiction and Substance Abuse says the key is being a "hands-on" parent. What is a "hands-on" parent? Well, there's a list of twelve things, and a "hands-on" parent does at least ten of them.

"Hands-on" parents: monitor their kids' TV viewing, monitor their internet use, put restrictions on which CDs their kids buy, know where their kids are after school, keep track of their kids on weekends, give regular chores to their children, are very aware of their teens' grades, have a curfew, eat dinner together most every night—without TV, have an adult in the house when their kids get home from school, know where their teen is, and tell their kids they won't tolerate any drug use.

Now, if you're a "hands-off" parent, your children are in trouble. Kids with "hands-off" parents are twice as likely to smoke, drink and do drugs.

So, especially for your kids, be a "hands-on" parent.

MY THOUGHTS:

Motherhood

NOT NOW, MOM!

Do you still get irritated at your mom?

Does your mother get on your nerves even though you're all grown up? Well, the next time she does something to bother you, think about this: what if she weren't around to do that anymore? Ah, then that chatter that can sound like nagging would be music to your ears. Her call that always seems to come just as you are walking out the door would be the most important conversation of your day. And her habit of giving you advice wouldn't be annoying, it would be comforting.

So if you still have your mom, be thankful and show her some extra special love today.

MY THOUGHTS:

_____

_____

_____

FAMILY MINUTES

HEALING WORDS

Not talking to someone you love?

Maybe it was just last week or maybe many years ago. Maybe something was said or something was done. It may have been your child or
one of your parents who wounded you deeply. You haven't spoken in
quite some time, and the wound is still there, open and festering. Or,
maybe you're the one who did the hurting. Why not call that person
today and ask for forgiveness whether or not you were the one at fault.
Don't qualify your apology. Just say it. Life on earth is too short to carry
a grudge.

Bring healing words to those you love.

MY THOUGHTS:

_____

_____

_____

IN PRAISE OF SINGLE MOMS

Single moms need twice the love this Mother's Day.

If being a mother is a labor of love, than being a single mother requires double the labor and double the love. Without a father around, single mothers have to give twice the hugs, twice the affection, and twice the attention with half the time, half the energy, and often half the resources. And no matter why these moms are doing the job of mothering on their own, we need to encourage them, especially for the sake of the children living in their homes.

All mothers have hopes and dreams for their children. Single mothers, however, have to do their hoping and dreaming on their own.

MY THOUGHTS:

129

May 9

ADOPTIVE MOMS

For some, Mother's Day can be a heartbreaking day.

While millions of moms will look into the eyes of their children and count their blessings, there are many other mothers who will only be able to wish they could look into those eyes. You see, these women gave their children up for adoption. For whatever reason, they made a decision to put the needs of their children ahead of their own. Just imagine a whisper on a mother's lips as she prays that her baby will find a loving home.

So if you are adopted, take a moment on Mother's Day to give thanks for your birth mother. Because even though she gave you away, she also gave you life.

MY THOUGHTS:

REMEMBERING MOM

Mother's Day will bring sadness for many.

Of course it's a wonderful way to honor Mom for all she has done. Yet, for those who have lost their mothers, it can be a sad day—especially if the loss is recent. So if you know someone who is without their mom, give them a call and tell them you just wanted to see how they are doing. Be willing to listen if they want to talk about their mother and what made her special.

Then, be thankful if you still have the blessing of a mother in your life.

MY THOUGHTS:

YOUR PRIORITIES

What are your priorities?

It's been said that we can know a lot about a person's priorities by looking at two things: their checkbook and their calendar. If our children were to look at our calendars, day planners or palm pilots, what would they see? A schedule filled with dinner meetings, parties and golf outings, or little league, dance rehearsals and school plays? We need to think about how we're spending our time. Then, on our calendars, mark specific blocks of time that we will spend with our children one-on-one doing what they want to do.

Time with our children should always be on our schedules.

MY THOUGHTS:

HUGS

A wonder drug that invigorates and rejuvenates without side effects is now available.

Yes, it's true. You can sleep better, reduce stress and help boost your immunity all in one easy step. What is this miracle drug? Hugging. That's right. Hugging. So write yourself a prescription. Start with at least five hugs a day for each of your children and your spouse. You don't need a special reason. Being in the same room is enough. If you're not a hugger, at first it may seem fake or unnatural to you. But what can it hurt? You've already been told how it can help you.

So reach out and add this wonder drug to your family's medicine cabinet.

MY THOUGHTS:

CHILDREN AND WORK

Want a great way to teach your children self-control?

Then teach them to work. But, you say, "Life is tough enough for our kids. I don't want to make it any more difficult for them." Well, not teaching our kids the value of work now may make things even more difficult for them later in life. You see, children who know how to work find it easier to control their impulses, to stay focused until a job is completed, to understand the connection between effort and opportunity, and to learn to manage money.

So teach your children to work. They'll be glad you did.

MY THOUGHTS:

TOO OLD TO READ TO?

Are your kids too old to read to?

When we think about reading to our kids, most of us think of young children, the ones who can't read yet or are just getting started. Well, you can read with your older kids too. But instead of picking out a book that can be read in one sitting, choose a longer book. Then set aside a regular reading time and take turns reading to each other. Reading a chapter a night helps build excitement and suspense.

For a recommended reading list for your kids, go to FamilyMinute.net.

MY THOUGHTS:

NONNEGOTIABLE DISCIPLINE

Do your kids try to negotiate their way out of discipline?

Some friends of mine disciplined their teenage daughter by taking the car away for the weekend. Well, she did not give up without a fight. She pleaded, she promised and she used every negotiating skill in the book. She said, "How about washing the car instead? How about washing and waxing the car?" Well, her parents stood firm. And that's the hard part. Many times we decide on a consequence and then feel like we're being too tough on our kids or they just wear us down.

But, remember, for discipline to work we need to stand our ground.

MY THOUGHTS:

CRYING

How do you handle crying in your family?

You've probably heard the old saying, "Big boys don't cry. Crying is for babies." Well, some experts say we shouldn't be too quick to talk our children out of their tears. Our first impulse might be to say things like, "Don't cry. It will be okay. You're a big girl now." But if our children are legitimately hurt or sad, that type of response teaches them to stifle their feelings. Instead, try saying, "I know that hurts. It's okay to cry."

Giving your kids permission to express their emotions will help them feel understood and accepted.

MY THOUGHTS:

FAMILY MINUTES

ACCEPT YOUR SPOUSE

Have your learned to accept your spouse?

We all know that you can't change someone unless they want to change. But boy do we try. We badger. We nag. We criticize. We just won't give up! Maybe your husband isn't the go-getter you thought he was going to be. Maybe your wife is more talkative than you'd like. Well, instead of dwelling on what they're not—and probably never will be—accept them as they are and adjust your expectations.

While your spouse may be different from your ideal, you'll never have peace until you practice acceptance.

MY THOUGHTS:

PAYNE STEWART

Shouldn't we all consider what people will say about us when we die?

After the plane crash that killed professional golfer Payne Stewart, people recalled his amazing career and trademark knickers. But the recollections went beyond that. *USA Today* wrote that in recent years "Stewart had become more content, and more at peace with himself," —more than any other time in his life. In fact, Stewart had recently credited his faith for those changes and for helping him focus on what was really important in life...his family and his relationship with God.

So, when you're gone, what will your family and friends say was important in your life?

MY THOUGHTS:

WEEDEATER

Want to turn yard work into a life lesson?

Recently I was doing some weeding with my three children. When I noticed them getting bored, I tossed out a question, "What would happen if we didn't weed?"

"Well," said my oldest daughter, "all the good stuff would die."

I went on to explain how that's true in our lives, and then had them tell me some of the weeds we all need to watch for. They came up with things like calling people names, lying and being mean to other children. We talked about how weeds choke out our joy and hurt our relationships.

It's just like in the yard, if we don't get rid of the weeds, the weeds will get rid of the good stuff.

MY THOUGHTS:

SINGLE PARENT SURVIVOR

If you think the people on the TV show "Survivor" have it tough, consider single parenting.

There's the "I'm the only person but I have to have three kids in three different parts of town at the same time" challenge. In the eating category it's the "Try to feed a family of four on a paycheck meant for one" competition. And, finally, the "twenty-four hour on call with no relief" endurance test. Now while it's every person for himself on the TV show, in real life it's okay to help single parents—with carpooling, fixing dinner or watching their kids.

So get in the game and help a single parent be more than a survivor.

MY THOUGHTS:

_____

_____

_____

TEMPERAMENTS

"I can't help it! That's just the way I am!"

Have you ever said that before? Those are the words often used to justify behavior or actions that are hurtful or insensitive. Now, even if you have a tendency to act a certain way, you can make changes. In his book *Why You Act the Way You Do*, Dr. Timothy LaHaye looks at the strengths and weaknesses of the four basic temperaments. He explains how you can overcome your weaknesses so you can perform better at work and get along with your spouse.

So tune up your temperament because you can help the way you act.

MY THOUGHTS:

_____

_____

_____

BABE RUTH

They called him hopeless, yet he became a hero.

He had eight siblings but was one of only two who survived into adulthood. His youth was spent in the rough part of Baltimore. In the end, his parents gave up on him and took him to an orphanage where he never had a visitor. He was called "incorrigible" and on his way to a sad life. But then someone intervened. A priest named Mathias stepped in. Mathias focused on the positive in the child instead of the negative. He encouraged instead of criticized. That grateful boy was Babe Ruth.

So how are you building up your children?

MY THOUGHTS:

_____

_____

_____

May 23

PASS THE PIGGY

Want to teach your kids manners without nagging?

Are you constantly asking your kids to chew with their mouths closed, put their napkins on their laps and keep their elbows off the table? Then try Pass the Piggy. First, get a picture of a pig (download one at FamilyMinute.net). Then, during meals, if someone reaches across the table or talks with their mouth full, they get the piggy. Whoever winds up with the pig at the end of the meal has to do the dishes.

We played it at my house, and guess who got stuck with the pig? That's right—I did. And the kids loved it.

MY THOUGHTS:

_____

_____

_____

SPY KIDS

The following marriage advice comes from the movie *Spy Kids*.

Toward the end of the movie, the young girl Carmen says, "Spy work, that's easy. Keeping a family together, that's difficult. And, that's a mission worth fighting for." Well, as a husband or wife it may be your darkest hour. Your spouse just told you she's leaving you; pornographic addiction may be clouding your marriage; your husband has become an alcoholic. Now, however, is not the time to surrender.

Continue to fight for your marriage. That's a mission worth fighting for.

MY THOUGHTS:

LEAVE IT AT THE OFFICE

Had a bad day at the office?

Work can be stressful. But for our children's sake, we need to leave that stress at the office. In one study, children talked about that very issue. An 11-year-old boy said, " If your work is too stressful, take a vacation, and don't take it out on your family." At the very least, before you walk in the door at home, take a deep breath and switch into parenting mode.

In the words of a 15-year-old girl, "I know that you're tired and stressed when coming home from work, but we need attention, affection and love." She's got that right.

Just because you had a bad day at the office doesn't mean you can't have a good night with your family!

MY THOUGHTS:

LOVE YOUR KIDS THROUGH THEIR MOM

Do you know one of the most important things you can do to be a better dad?

Is it taking your kids to the zoo, reading them a bedtime story or having daily talks? Believe it or not, loving your children's mother is absolutely the best thing you can do. Why? Well, a husband and wife who let their kids know they're in love provide a secure, safe environment for their children. Here's what a child thinks, "If Dad and Mom accept each other and are happy with each other, then home is a safe place and a sure thing." A father who shows kindness to his wife is seen as a true protector of his family.

So, Dad, before you reach out to your kids, first reach out to your wife.

MY THOUGHTS:

FAMILY MINUTES

FIGHTING AND KIDS

If you fight in front of your kids, you need to stop.

It's okay for our children to see us working through differences in a calm manner. Conflict is natural. But it should not move into fighting, especially when our children are around. That means no screaming, no name calling, no slamming doors or throwing things. And, there should be absolutely no physical threats or violence. This kind of arguing scares children. It not only makes them feel unsafe, but it is a bad example of resolving conflict.

So while controlled discussions are okay, fighting is not.

MY THOUGHTS:

MONOPOLY

Do you remember playing Monopoly when you were a kid?

You bought properties like Boardwalk and Park Place. Then mom said it was time for dinner, and the game was over. Your money, hotels and houses were gone. You know, life is like that. You spend years getting "stuff." Then, one day, your life is over. Your greatest legacy won't be the material things you leave behind. Those will fade away. Instead, it will be the lives you've touched, the relationships you've built, your children and grandchildren.

That legacy will endure after the game ends.

MY THOUGHTS:

RECEIVING GIFTS

Want to make your spouse feel really bad?

The next time they give you a gift say something like, "You shouldn't have spent good money on flowers." Or, "I didn't need another tie." How about, "I told you not to buy me anything else. I already have everything I need." Ouch! Think about how that must make them feel. Instead, shower them with appreciation. If you're not exactly crazy about what they bought you, still let them know you're genuinely grateful for their thoughtfulness.

So the next time your spouse comes bearing gifts, just say thanks.

MY THOUGHTS:

KIDS UNDER PRESSURE

When's the last time your child had a meltdown?

You're at the grocery store with your sweet little son or daughter when all of a sudden they fall to the floor and start kicking and screaming. Well, before you start disciplining, think about this: young children up to about 9 years old don't always know how to express their feelings. When they're tired or hungry, they may act aggressively; have a temper tantrum; or whine. And maybe we've filled their day with more than they can handle. We've run them ragged.

So to avoid a meltdown, pull back before you regret pushing too hard.

MY THOUGHTS:

T-SHIRT QUILT

Hey, Mom, save that T-ball shirt and that soccer jersey!

A *Family Minute* listener has a great idea for recording your children's sports history. She keeps her kids' uniforms and uses them to make T-shirt quilts. First, she cuts the shirts into squares and irons them onto fusible interfacing. Then she sews the squares together until the quilt gets to be just the size she wants. What a great gift for your child's graduation or season-ending celebration.

So save those shirts, pull out your scissors and do some simple sewing for a keepsake your children will treasure for a lifetime.

MY THOUGHTS:

IN HIS OWN WORDS

Wouldn't it be nice to go back in time and feel what your parents felt when raising you?

A friend of mine is creating a legacy for his daughters. Every couple of weeks he pulls out two notebooks and writes a letter to each of his girls. He shares the struggles and joys that go along with being a father and husband. When his girls are grown, he will give them those pages of life. And from those pages they'll understand that although their dad wasn't perfect, he did the best job he could. They'll also have a blueprint for parenting their own children as they read about the challenges and triumphs life sends everyone's way.

Finally, they'll see that their father loved them enough to put his feelings into words.

MY THOUGHTS:

FAMILY CONSTITUTION

Do you have a family constitution?

This constitution basically outlines what you and your family believe in, stand for and expect from one another. When you're ready to write your constitution, get everyone together and be ready to spend an hour or two on the project. Include the areas of faith, family, friends and finances. Write down how you'll include worship in your lives. Spell out how you will show your love to one another. Include a line or two on how your family will serve others. Finally, talk about finances and how you'll save, give and spend your money.

When you're finished display it, study it and live by it.

MY THOUGHTS:

_____

_____

_____

General Marriage

THE ONE-ISSUE RULE

Do you know about the one-issue rule and why you need it?

Your spouse starts getting on you for running late. So you say, "Well, if I had a clean pair of socks to wear, I wouldn't be late!" You change the focus completely. Whoa! That's called getting sidetracked, which can lead to an even bigger fight. Now's the time to use the phrase "stick to the issue" to refocus and reel yourselves back to the original topic. Focus on that matter alone until you resolve it.

Problems can be solved when you tackle one issue at a time.

MY THOUGHTS:

FAMILY MINUTES

GRANDKID CAMP

Are your grandchildren miles away?

If they are, you can still have a great relationship. And one of the best ways to make that happen is to have a "grandkid" camp. A man who's now in his thirties says some of his best memories are of the two weeks he'd spend with his grandmother and cousins every summer. She'd prepare their special rooms, put out the slip n' slide and fix all their favorite foods. Just those annual two weeks helped build loving relationships that are still strong today.

So schedule your own grandkid camp and let the fun begin.

MY THOUGHTS:

TOO EASY ON YOUR TEEN?

Is the good life making your teenager soft?

When school's out teenagers stay up late, hang out with their friends or spend hours talking on the phone. Then they sleep half the day away. In the meantime, mom's cutting the grass, dad's giving them money and they have no responsibilities. Sure, kids need downtime. But if you let them off easy, you're actually hurting them. Encourage them to show responsibility by helping them learn it. Have them get a part-time job. Give them regular chores, and don't do everything for them.

In the end, having it too easy will make things tougher for your kids.

MY THOUGHTS:

FAMILY MINUTES

BABY-SITTER CHECKLIST

Does your baby-sitter have all of the information she needs?

It's Friday night and you and your wife have a hot date. Just as you're about to run out the door you remember to tell the baby-sitter where you'll be and your cell phone number. But there's other information she needs too. She should have the neighbors' phone numbers, your exact street address and when to call 911. Write out your own checklist or download a free one from our website, FamilyMinute.net.

Make sure you give your baby-sitter all of the information she needs, and you'll get peace of mind in return.

MY THOUGHTS:

FAMOUS FATHER: THE GENERAL

Dads, are you making a difference in your child's life?

Let me tell you the story of Luther. He was a confident man, small in stature but large in love. He lived in the South Bronx of New York and supported his wife and kids with jobs as a gardener and a shipping clerk. He left his children a legacy of good character and hard work. Luther's son says this: "I wouldn't be where I am today without my father." Who is Luther's son? His name is General Colin Powell.

Dads, you hold the power to make a difference in your child's life. Give of your time and yourself to make that difference a positive one.

MY THOUGHTS:

FAMOUS FATHER: THE PRIME MINISTER

Dads, are you sharing wisdom with your children?

Alfred Roberts was a shopkeeper in a small town. He was a fountain of wisdom and knowledge for his daughter, Margaret, even though he had little formal education. Margaret clearly remembers a time when she wanted to go out and play with her friends instead of doing her homework. But her father told her, "Never do things just because other people do them." He impressed her with these words. Although it was a simple expression, she carries it with her to this day. The daughter's name is Margaret Thatcher, former British Prime Minister.

Take the time to share your wisdom with your children. Your carefully chosen words today may impress them for a lifetime.

MY THOUGHTS:

Fatherhood

FAMOUS FATHER: THE GENERAL

Dads, how can you inspire courage in your kids?

There once was a father who as a district attorney was a busy man. Yet, he adored his kids and not only took them fishing and sailing, but spent extra time reading with his son. The boy was dyslexic and would come home from school crying because he couldn't read very well. Wiping away his son's tears, the father talked to him about courage and how it could help him get through the tough times. The child learned the lesson well. You see, that boy later helped lead the world through one of its most challenging times. His name was George—now known to the world as General George S. Patton.

Dads, the courage you instill in your children today may prepare them for courageous acts tomorrow.

MY THOUGHTS:

FAMOUS FATHER: THE PREACHER

Dads, the way you handle tough times will influence your children.

Frank had a small dairy farm in North Carolina. His kids' memories include seeing him walk up the hot, dusty path back to the farmhouse. In the 1929 stock market crash, Frank lost his entire life savings—$4,000. But his son William remembers how his dad did not lose his faith, "My dad never complained about life...and was always hopeful about the future." William, known to us as Billy Graham, credits his father with teaching him about practical faith.

So what are you teaching your children when you go through tough times?

MY THOUGHTS:

DAD—IT'S NEVER TOO LATE

Is it ever too late to be a good father?

Maybe you weren't there for your kids when they were little. Maybe you made bad choices that are still affecting their lives. Maybe your kids live at home, but you already feel they've slipped away. Well, no matter how much polluted water has gone under the bridge, don't give up. Reach out to your children. Maybe they need to hear you say you're sorry and you love them. And maybe you need to back up those words with actions.

Become the father you know you should be and the father your children—no matter their age—still need you to be.

MY THOUGHTS:

FAMILY MINUTES

A PARENT'S FORGIVENESS

Are you a parent who is troubled over a broken relationship with your child?

Ernest Hemingway wrote about a Spanish father and son whose relationship was shattered. When the rebellious son ran away, the father placed an ad in the paper saying, "Paco, please meet me in front of the newspaper office at noon. All is forgiven. Love, Father." He was amazed the next day when 800 sons, all named Paco, showed up seeking reconciliation with their fathers.

If you are facing a strained relationship with one of your kids, maybe today is the day for you to reach out to him or her with love and forgiveness.

MY THOUGHTS:

ROUGH AND TUMBLE

Dads, what family fun do you create in your home?

A friend of mine says a favorite memory of her father is how he would let her draw on his back. No, not with pens or markers, but with her finger. She would draw a picture and he would try to guess what it was. At my house I'm the "tickle monster." I chase the kids around the house, playfully tackle them to the ground, and get big laughs when the tickle monster attacks. You see, those are the times that build memories and strengthen the bond between father and child.

So make sure you're adding to the family fun in your home. You may even like being the "tickle monster."

MY THOUGHTS:

FAMILY MINUTES

PARENTING YOUR SPOUSE?

Are you treating your spouse like a child?

Once you have kids, it's easy to stay in the parenting mode all the time. Pretty soon you're talking to your mate the same way you talk to your children. One minute you're telling your kids to clean their room and do their homework. A few moments later you're rattling off a list of things to your mate in the same tone of voice. As busy as families are these days it's easy to fall into that habit. But we need to make an effort to deal with our spouse adult to adult.

After all, in marriage, most of us want a partner—not a parent.

MY THOUGHTS:

_____

_____

_____

PHOTO FIELD TRIP

Want to make some lasting memories this summer?

Pick up some inexpensive disposable cameras for your kids. Then decide on a photography theme. Maybe it's animals, interesting buildings or friends. Next, search out a location where you can find lots of possibilities, and let the kids snap away. When all of the film is used, get it developed. Then have the kids make a scrapbook of their photographs with written descriptions of each shot.

Your children will not only enjoy taking the pictures, they'll have lasting memories of their summer vacation.

MY THOUGHTS:

MARRIAGE GREETING

How do you greet your spouse?

You're standing at the kitchen sink when he walks in the front door. Do you holler out, "I'm back here!" Or maybe you're sitting in your favorite chair reading the paper when she gets home. Do you mumble over your sports section, "Hey." Well, try instead to make a habit of greeting your spouse at the door. Whoever arrives home first gets to make the move. When you hear your spouse open the door, stop what you're doing, walk over to them and give them an enthusiastic hug.

A greeting will not only make them feel great, it may even melt away some of the tension of the day.

MY THOUGHTS:

HOME IMPROVEMENT

Are you ready for a home improvement project?

The best way to improve your home life is to spend more time together as a family. But for this home improvement project to work, you have to make it a priority. So be creative. Try scheduling in a weekly game night. Eat as many meals together as you can. Try for at least a couple of dinners a week and add in other meals as you go. And on the weekend, save at least one day just for family fun.

Use the tool of time for a home improvement project well worth the effort.

MY THOUGHTS:

FAMILY MINUTES

PHONE YOUR WIFE

Men, do you know the power of a phone call?

As a general rule, most men, unless they're in the dating phase, don't really like to talk on the phone. To most of us it's strictly for getting or receiving information. Well, guys, I have a news flash for you: women like it when their husbands call just to say "hello." The call accomplishes a couple of things. It lets your wife know you're thinking about her, and it shows you care about how her day is going. It doesn't have to be a long conversation. Just tell her you called to say you love her.

So pick up the phone and reach out to your wife.

MY THOUGHTS:

_____

_____

_____

CHILDREN AND WAR

Are you comfortable talking to your kids about war?

Even if your children act like they're not bothered by war, you should still approach them and give them a chance to talk. Many times kids will keep their feelings inside and try to figure things out on their own. So let them know you're there to listen. Ask them how they feel, answer their questions honestly and share your feelings. If they seem troubled, spend more time with them than usual.

Practice your faith as a family. Pray. Compassionately reassure them of your love and care. And let them know that they have a safe place at home.

MY THOUGHTS:

171

CAMPING LESSONS

Is your idea of camping stopping at the nearest hotel?

Well, you're not alone. Many of my friends feel the same way. But when I took my wife and three young children camping, we learned a valuable lesson from this outdoor experience: it's great for family building. You'll enjoy a home-cooked meal *together*, even if it's just beanie weenies. You'll work *together* putting up the tent, making s'mores and collecting firewood. And you'll brave the elements *together*—mosquitoes, the cold and torrential downpours. Did you catch the key word there? *Together*.

So round up the kids, bypass that hotel and head for your campsite.

MY THOUGHTS:

HUSBAND HELPERS

Can your husband do anything right?

I don't want to get myself into trouble, but a lot of wives act like their husbands can't do anything. When he tries to change the baby's diaper, she corrects him and takes over. When she asks him to help with the kitchen, he barely gets started before she steps in and says she'll finish it. Then she wonders why she has to do "everything."

Well, the point is, when your husband offers to help or responds to your request for help, let him do the job his own way. As long as it's not a life-or-death situation, be glad for the assistance and just say "thanks."

MY THOUGHTS:

_____

_____

_____

June 22

FAMILY MINUTES

KIDS AT THE NEIGHBOR'S

Your child is at a neighbor's house—do you know what they're watching?

When your kids are at home you can monitor what video games they're playing and what movies they're watching. But when they're at your neighbor's, it can be a challenge. Tell your neighbors that for your young children only G-rated movies and non-violent video games are allowed. And as your kids get older, make sure they know what you consider acceptable. My kids need permission before they watch any movie beyond PG or play any video game with violence.

For your kids' safety, keep up your neighborhood watch.

MY THOUGHTS:

LETTING GO

Letting go is sometimes the only way to hang on.

A little boy named Timmy reached into an expensive vase to grab a penny. Then, his hand got stuck, and he could not get it out. Before resorting to smashing the vase, Timmy's father said, "Son, let's try one more time. Hold your fingers straight out, and I'll pull."

But Timmy said, "I can't do that, Daddy. I'll drop my penny."

How many times have we hung onto unimportant things like grudges or hurt feelings and ended up risking something even more valuable? Sometimes letting go is the best way to get something even greater in return.

MY THOUGHTS:

June 24

FAMILY MINUTES

MINUTE BY MINUTE

Having a hard time getting your kids to read?

If your kids are past the "read to me" stage, you'll need to try a different approach. One way is to set "minute milestones." Set up a chart and have your kids record how many minutes they read each day. You might want to set a 10-minute daily minimum. Then, each time they hit the 100-minute mark, do something special or give them a reward. You can also apply this approach by keeping track of the number of books they read. Set a goal and a deadline.

Agree on a reward for reaching the mark, and let the reading begin.

MY THOUGHTS:

MAN OF STEEL AND VELVET

Are you a man of steel and velvet?

Poet Carl Sandburg once described Abraham Lincoln as a man of steel and velvet. He was referring to the unique combination of Lincoln's strong qualities—integrity, honesty and courage—and his softer qualities—compassion, friendliness and love for others. To be a man of steel and velvet like Abraham Lincoln, a man cannot place too much emphasis on either his steel side or his velvet side.

It is having a perfect balance of strength and compassion that can make a man a better husband and father. A man of steel and velvet.

MY THOUGHTS:

MAN OF THE HOUSE

It's a trap any single parent can fall into.

When a spouse leaves, it's easy to turn our children into little adults. The oldest son becomes "the man of the house," and the oldest daughter becomes her parent's best friend and shoulder to cry on. There's nothing wrong with sharing our struggles with our children and giving them more responsibility. Still, single parents need to make sure they let their kids be kids. Your kids need to feel like they can depend on you, not the other way around.

So if you're a single parent, avoid the trap of giving your children more than they can handle.

MY THOUGHTS:

_____

_____

_____

FAMILY DINNERS

Family dinners nourish ties with teens.

According to a study out of Cincinnati Children's Hospital Center, adolescents whose parents eat dinner with them five times per week or more are the least likely to be on drugs, to be depressed or to be in trouble with the law. And the most important ingredient is not what's on the dinner table. Whether it's a home-cooked meal or pizza delivery, the ingredient that does make the difference is regularly setting aside time to eat and talk together. Family mealtimes provide a centerpiece for family traditions. And it's also a great way to impart our faith to our children.

Clearly, there is power in breaking bread together.

MY THOUGHTS:

_____

_____

_____

June 28

MOM, MOM, MOM

If you have kids then you know how it feels to be "mommed" all day long.

Responding to every one of those calls and tugs can feel overwhelming. But think about this: before long that seemingly unending well of "moms" will dry up. It won't be long before your kids are out the door, at school all day, getting their driver's license or heading off to college.

So when you think you can't bear one more request, realize that one day you'll actually long to hear that little voice saying that precious word, "Mom."

MY THOUGHTS:

ARE WE THERE YET?

Want to make your family vacation more fun and less stressful?

I'm sure parents can easily picture this: you're on vacation, driving down the road, and from the backseat for the five hundredth time you hear, "Are we there yet?" Well, getting there can be half the fun. All it takes is a little planning. First, get the kids involved. Before you head out, call a family meeting to plan your route. Assign a map reader, a snack coordinator, a hotel expert, a restaurant spotter and someone to show you points of interest. Don't let your kids isolate themselves with beeping game machines or headsets.

Make your family vacation a family memory.

MY THOUGHTS:

TITLE OR TESTIMONY?

Do you have a title or a testimony?

One of these days all of us are going to die. And when you do, what will others say about you? Will they talk about your title or your testimony? Will you just have the title doctor, attorney, businessman or will you have a testimony of a man who put his family first? Will you just have a title of scratch golfer or tennis pro or a testimony of someone who served the community? Will you just have the title father or a testimony of a dad who loved his wife and prepared his children to impact the world for good?

Do you have a title or a testimony?

MY THOUGHTS:

_____

_____

_____

FAMILY MINUTES

COME SAIL AWAY

Is your marriage shipshape or sinking?

I've always enjoyed the beauty of sailboats. Above the waterline is the sleek hull and flowing sails. But it's what you don't see that really counts. Beneath the water you have the ballast, the heavy material that gives the boat stability. Well, there are marriages that appear strong on the surface but have no substance to keep them from capsizing when the storms of life hit. What gives your marriage stability—is it the fear of being alone, social pressure, the kids? Or is it mutual faith, life-long commitment and unconditional love?

Make sure your marriage has those things that will keep it sailing for life.

MY THOUGHTS:

LET THEM GO

In the movie *The Patriot* there is a battle within a battle.

The Mel Gibson movie is set during the Revolutionary War, a time of major conflict. Yet, there's also an ongoing battle of wills between the dad, played by Gibson, and his teenage son. The boy wants to become a soldier. His father doesn't want him to. But Gibson's character has to learn a lesson shared by all parents—when a child is in his older teenage years, the job of "parenting by controlling" is done.

That's why it's so important to teach our children well along the way. So when they do go off on their own, they'll know how to fight—and win—their own battles.

MY THOUGHTS,

INDEPENDENCE DAY

Go back to the Fourth of July 1776.

On that day 56 men signed a document that would change the course of the world—The Declaration of Independence. It says, "We hold these truths to be self-evident: That all men are created equal; that they are endowed by their Creator with certain unalienable rights; that among these are life, liberty, and the pursuit of happiness." Thomas Jefferson penned those words. And since they were written, thousands of patriots have given their lives to defend that ideal. Do your children know the story behind the signing of the Declaration of Independence? Do you?

Take a break this Independence Day from the fireworks and cookouts to talk with your kids about the people who secured the freedom we enjoy today. Let's remember their sacrifice.

MY THOUGHTS:

FAMILY MINUTES

YOUR GIRL IS GROWING UP

So your daughter doesn't want to hold your hand?

Sometime between 8 and 12 years of age your little girl may pull away from you when you grab her hand in public. I realize that it will break your heart when it happens. It did mine. But don't freak out. She may just be at that preadolescent stage when she is becoming more aware of those around her and more concerned about how she looks and acts.

So try not to totally embarrass her in public, especially you, Dad. Just keep loving her, hugging her and connecting with her every time you can.

MY THOUGHTS:

VIDEO GAME REVIEW

You've heard it before, "Hey, Mom, can I get a new video game? I just gotta have that new video game!"

Now what do you do? You're not in the mood for a battle. So, just this time, you give in and let your son or daughter get a game you know nothing about. Well, you're not alone. One study shows that only 40 percent of parents make a habit of looking at ratings before buying or renting a video game. Unfortunately, the most popular games out there are extremely violent.

So the next time your kids want a video game, review it first. If you don't have time for that, tell them the video adventure will just have to wait.

MY THOUGHTS:

General
Parenting

JUST FOR TODAY

Mom, Dad, will you try something for your children just for today?

Just for today forget about the laundry and take them to the park. Unplug the telephone, turn off the computer and sit with them and blow bubbles. Just for today let them wear what they want and smile and say how perfect it is. Skip your favorite TV shows and snuggle beside them for hours. Let them stay up late so you can count the stars with them.

Just for today think about the mothers and fathers who no longer have their children, and be thankful you have yours.

MY THOUGHTS:

PARENTS' TIRADES

Ever seen someone lose their temper with their child?

Recently I was in the checkout line and saw a mother lose her temper with her preschooler. The child was just being a child—fidgeting and saying, "Mommy, let's go." Well, you could tell the mother was worn out. She snapped. She pushed the child and cursed at her. The behavior was inexcusable. As parents we need to have self-control, even when we're tired and frustrated.

While it may require extra prayer and patience on our part, we should do our best to treat our children gently and lovingly—no matter what.

MY THOUGHTS:

OVERWEIGHT KIDS AND TV

Is your child a little on the heavy side?

It is well-known that carrying extra weight around isn't healthy for kids. But before you make radical changes in your child's diet, consider that one of the most fattening things in your home could be your TV. You see, the weight problem could really be a TV problem. One study found that when kids cut back on TV time they lose weight. It makes sense doesn't it? Less TV time usually means more physical activity and less munching. So turn off that TV! Take a walk together. Go outside, play tag or throw a ball.

In other words, to weigh less—watch less.

MY THOUGHTS:

_____

_____

_____

MERCENARY OR WARRIOR

Are you a mercenary or a warrior?

A mercenary fights to make money for his own benefit. He is basically devoted to himself. Picture the businessman who works seventy hours a week looking for the next big deal and financial payoff. He says he's doing it for his family, but they don't buy it. The warrior, on the other hand, fights for a purpose greater than himself—a higher calling. He's the guy who balances job and home life. He works to provide for his family and those less fortunate than himself.

So, are you a mercenary or a warrior?

MY THOUGHTS:

FAMILY MINUTES

MUSIC LESSONS

Does your child have music in his life?

I don't mean just listening to it. I mean the study of music. Every child should get the chance to explore his musical abilities. Music can teach discipline and build confidence, especially in kids who might not excel at physical activities or traditional academics. If you can afford private lessons, go that route. If not, see what the school system offers in band, chorus or orchestra. Check out community programs too.

Introduce your child to the joy of music. Who knows, you might just have a Mozart or a Faith Hill in the making.

MY THOUGHTS:

DISCIPLINE—THE 3 R's

Do you know the three R's of discipline? Here they are: remove, reflect and reconnect. When you need to discipline, immediately remove your child from the situation, whether it's fighting with siblings or name calling. Removing is not timeout. The goal is to give your child time to think about what he has done. It also gives everyone involved time to calm down and prepare to reflect—the second R.

Ask your child what he did wrong. Don't let him make excuses or blame others. Next, ask him why it was wrong and how he'll act differently next time. This is where you focus on your child's motives. You want to shape his heart so he'll be self-motivated to change his behavior. Once you've discussed the problem, tell your child the consequences for his actions.

The third R is extremely important—reconnect. Make sure the bond between you and your child is not broken. Tell him you love him unconditionally, give him a hug and let him know you believe in his ability to make the right decision next time.

The three R's of discipline: remove, reflect and reconnect.

MY THOUGHTS:

THE LONG VIEW

If you need your eyes checked, see an optometrist, but if you want your vision checked, see a grandparent.

As parents it's so easy to see only what's in front of us and then react in a way that often makes matters worse. Why not check in with someone who's been down the parenting road before? Grandparents can offer insights that will help us see the bigger picture and find a more lasting solution. When department store millionaire JC Penney turned 95 years old, he said, "My eyesight may be getting weaker, but my vision is increasing."

Grandparents have an experience advantage, and we'd be wise to check out the view from their perspective.

MY THOUGHTS:

BITTERNESS BUG

Are you infecting your children with the bug of bitterness?

Well, think about this. Do you hold grudges? Do you have a chip on your shoulder? Do you go around whining about how your boss is unfair or how your ex did you wrong? If you do, then be prepared to have your children catch your sour attitude. Pretty soon they'll be blaming everybody and everything for their troubles instead of taking on responsibilities themselves. You see, kids pick up on our attitudes. They mimic our methods of handling life.

So work on getting rid of your own bitterness, or else be prepared to see your children bitter too.

MY THOUGHTS:

FAMILY MINUTES

DON'T RETREAT!

When the going gets tough, do you just go?

Okay, let me set the scene. You're in an argument with your spouse and things are reaching the boiling point. So, instead of standing the heat, you get out of the kitchen. In other words, you walk away without saying anything...withdraw...retreat. Now that's okay if you say something like, "Honey, I need a few minutes to cool off. I'll be back." Or, "Can we set a time to talk about this later?" But when you just walk away, you leave behind an angrier and more frustrated spouse, which can cause even more trouble.

Remember, shutdowns can quickly lead to showdowns.

MY THOUGHTS:

DATING AND THE SINGLE PARENT

Should a single parent mix family life and dating life?

You're dating someone you really like and want your child to meet them. So they meet, and you all start hanging out. Then, the relationship ends. The cycle can be repeated over and over, and that's not good for your child. Children become attached. And if they have people popping in and out of their lives, they'll have a hard time feeling secure in their relationships.

So don't bring someone into your child's life unless you're contemplating marriage. It may take some extra effort and planning, but it's worth it to protect your child.

MY THOUGHTS:

_____

_____

_____

FAMILY MINUTES

UNDIVIDED ATTENTION

How often does your child get your undivided attention?

Too many kids don't get it enough. When they're home, their parents are talking on the phone, watching TV or reading. In the car, the radio is on or that phone is back in the picture. Some parents half listen while doing other things: cleaning, going through paperwork or fixing dinner.

Of course you can't give your undivided attention all of the time, but you can make a point to stop what you're doing, look your child in the eye and make him or her feel like they're the most important thing in your world. Because, after all, they are.

MY THOUGHTS:

TEENS AND DEPRESSION

Do you know how to help your teenager avoid depression?

The teen years can bring some tough emotional struggles. Most kids want to be popular and well-liked. If that doesn't happen, they often turn inward and withdraw into depression. Well, the *Journal of Youth and Adolescence* says that religious worship significantly reduces depression among teenagers. It gets kids connected to something outside of themselves. Another study found that taking part in religious services can help with the transition to college by improving students' mental health.

So offer your child the benefits of worship. Because when you're a teenager, every bit helps.

MY THOUGHTS:

SNEAK ATTACKS

"If this marriage is supposed to be so good, then why do I sometimes feel so bad?"

Have you ever thought that? If so, your marriage may be the victim of what Dr. Les Parrott calls "sneak attacks"—things that sneak into a marriage like an unsuspecting lion. And a big one is busyness. Much of our busyness results from an over-booked calendar. We are responsible for our calendar and, therefore, our own busyness. So review your calendar each week with your spouse. Set a regular date night, maybe even a getaway weekend.

Mark it on your calendar and don't let anything interfere.

MY THOUGHTS:

_____

_____

_____

A FATHER'S LOVE

Imagine training your whole life for the Olympics.

That's what Derek Redmond did. And in 1992 he finally had his chance at gold. He lined up for his race on the track. When the starting gun fired, he tore past the other runners. But then he fell to the ground. He had pulled a hamstring. As he struggled to get up, a man appeared by his side. It was his father, who had been watching from the stands as his son faltered. He rushed through the crowd and onto the track to help his child. Lifting the sobbing athlete, he and Derek hobbled across the finish line together.

Fathers, always be there for your children, but especially when they stumble.

MY THOUGHTS:

July 20

FAMILY MINUTES

VIOLENT VIDEO GAMES

Do you think violent video games are harmless?

Lieutenant Colonel David Grossman wrote the book, *Stop Teaching Our Kids to Kill*, which is about how people learn to kill. He says that when kids play violent video games, they are desensitizing themselves to killing. Grossman also says that every time a child plays a point-and-shoot type of video game, he is learning the exact reflex and motor skills needed for shooting someone in real life. Parents, educate yourselves on what games are out there. Then get with your kids and agree upon what's acceptable and what's not.

Together, you and your children can be the first line of defense against the impact of violent video games.

MY THOUGHTS:

_____

_____

_____

DADS AND HUGS

Dads, when was the last time you hugged your children?

If your kids are small, you probably hug them a lot. But once they reach that adolescent stage, they might not seem as interested in a hug from old Dad. Don't let that stop you. Now, they might not want a big hug from you in front of their friends, but there are other times and places that are perfect—when you see them after work or before they go to bed. Believe me, even big kids need reassuring, physical contact with their fathers.

So get past their rolling eyes and "Aw, Dad," and hug away.

MY THOUGHTS:

GRIN AND BEAR IT

Unless you choose your battles, raising a teenager can seem like World War Three every day.

We all know that teenagers can have some pretty crazy ideas. After all, we were young once too, right? So instead of having a showdown every day, only go head-to-head on those issues that have real moral or social significance. They might include drugs, drinking or sex. But, parents, we need to try, yes try being the key word, not to get worked up about typical teenage phases—odd clothes, different hair styles or junk food diets.

Adolescence will bring enough big issues, so don't waste your energy on the little ones.

MY THOUGHTS:

R-E-S-T IN MARRIAGE

Do you want to put conflict to rest in your marriage?

Here's a formula to help you. Take the letters in the word REST. Start with R for review the problem. Discuss the problem and pinpoint clearly what the issue is. Don't try to jump ahead to solving the problem—that comes later. And when you're having your discussion use the drive-through communication method. That's where only one person speaks at a time, and then the other repeats back what they heard, just like at a drive-through restaurant.

Once you've both agreed on what the specific issue is, move onto E for evaluate options. Discuss the different ways the problem can be resolved. Try to have an unselfish attitude as you look at the pros and cons of each option.

Now you're ready for S—solve the problem. Agree on an option and put it into action.

Finally, T is for track your progress. Set a specific time to sit down and talk about how things are going. Don't be discouraged if things haven't gone perfectly. Instead, regroup and address the issue again.

Make adjustments if you need to and put your conflicts to REST.

MY THOUGHTS:

FAMILY MINUTES

DAD POWER

Dads, how much time have you spent with your children this week?

Okay, was it ten hours, ten minutes or not at all? Not to put you on a guilt trip, but as dads we need to know the sobering facts. Violent criminals are overwhelmingly males who grew up without fathers: the statistics show that 70 percent of long-term prison inmates and 72 percent of adolescent murderers fit into that category. So let's commit to spending time with our children one-on-one, really listening to them and doing what they want to do. They need our guidance and we need to give it to them.

Remember, it's our responsibility as dads to guide and love our kids.

MY THOUGHTS:

BE FIRM—NOT HARSH

Some parents think the only way to be firm is to be harsh.

Harshness uses angry words and emotions to try to make children obey. But firmness shows that a boundary is secure and can't be crossed without a consequence. Here's how it works: your son turns on the TV after you've told him to go to bed. Instead of yelling or getting into a debate, you say, "Son, you know the consequence for disobedience." Now if your son wants to argue, don't take the bait. Calmly remind him that he has crossed a boundary, then leave it at that.

Be firm—not harsh. It works.

MY THOUGHTS:

_____

_____

_____

OLYMPIC MATERIAL?

Is your child Olympic material?

Most of the Olympic athletes didn't declare at birth, "Hey, Mom and Dad, I'm going to compete in the Olympics!" No, the road to the Olympics usually starts with a child who has talent and parents who take the time to notice it and nurture it.

Be involved with your own kids enough to encourage them to pursue their interests and hobbies. While they might not ever make the Olympic team, they'll benefit from the discipline and joy that comes from pursuing and excelling at something they love.

MY THOUGHTS:

THINK BEFORE YOU DIVORCE

If you're considering divorce, read this.

Divorce is tough on kids. Judith Wallerstein and her colleagues say in their book, *The Unexpected Legacy of Divorce*, that children of divorce can face an uphill battle. Overall, they are more likely to abuse drugs and alcohol. And girls from divorced families often start having premarital sex at an earlier age. As a group, children of divorce might hold their own in the workplace, but suffer more in social relationships. So what's the message? While divorce is sometimes inevitable, before you consider it, try giving your marriage another try.

Think of your children and their future.

MY THOUGHTS:

_____

_____

_____

DARE TO BE DIFFERENT

Singer Mandy Moore dares to be different.

For teens, the pressure to conform can be significant. They want to be just like everyone else—do what they do, say what they say, wear what they wear, and go where they go. Conformity, however, can be dangerous. It can cause our teens to do things they know are wrong. That's what happens when they just want to "fit in." But Mandy Moore says there is power in being different. In fact, she doesn't sport any tattoos or piercing or revealing clothes. And her songs generally do not contain questionable lyrics.

So dare your kids to be different. Others will soon follow.

MY THOUGHTS:

TOO BUSY OR TOO MUCH TV?

Are you really "too busy" or just not using your time wisely?

Consider this: one study showed that adults who said their lives were just "too busy" were actually watching ten hours of TV a week. Think about what you could get done in ten hours. It's like having a whole extra day. And if you don't think you watch that much television, keep a TV log for seven days just to be sure. You might be surprised at what you find.

The bottom line is this: watching too much TV can keep you from connecting with your spouse and your children. So stay busy with what really matters.

MY THOUGHTS:

DADDY'S LITTLE ANGEL

Ever thought about grounding your teenage daughter until she was like—28 years old?

Remember when your little angel would run to meet you at the door or when she cried on your shoulder about her goldfish? Well, before long, she won't be leaning on you anymore. She'll be taking cues from classmates or even a boyfriend. But don't panic. Instead, prepare. Her attitude toward men will be shaped by her relationship with just one person—you. And if that relationship is strong, it will stand against all the peer pressure, all the hormones, and yes—even all the boyfriends.

Dads, take time now to listen, to learn and to love your daughter.

MY THOUGHTS:

_____

_____

_____

GRATITUDE-POWER

Do you know the power of a "thank you" in marriage?

After you've been with someone for a while it's easy to take them for granted. We just expect that they'll take out the garbage, make the bed, fix dinner, mow the lawn or get the kids dressed in the morning. Sound familiar? Well, try giving them some credit for those routine things. Write them a note of appreciation for their hard work or just say "thanks" for a job well done.

Give it a try, and you may see the big power a little "thank you" can have.

MY THOUGHTS:

JUST FIVE SECONDS

How much can you do in five seconds?

It all depends on how you use your time. A survivor of an earthquake in Taiwan a few years ago was telling a reporter about how the quake destroyed his home and left his family missing. "Within five seconds," he said, "everything around us shook, then everything, everyone was gone." Five short seconds. Imagine, in the time it takes you to reach for your alarm clock, your entire world could change! It's a good reminder to use our time wisely. So take five seconds to encourage your child, kiss your spouse or be thankful your family is still with you.

Five seconds. One day it may be all you've got.

MY THOUGHTS:

CHILDHOOD SMOKING

Have you heard about the power of the puff?

Although we know smoking can be addictive, a study shows just how easy it is to become addicted. The research found that some 12- and 13-year-olds became hooked on smoking after just a few cigarettes. That's right. And when they had to go without smoking they reported very grown-up symptoms such as irritability and anxiousness. The bottom line is that experimenting with smoking is not child's play.

As parents we need to teach our kids why smoking is harmful, so they won't have a future full of nicotine patches and pledges in order to quit.

MY THOUGHTS:

FAMILY MINUTES

FORGIVENESS-1

Do you know how to ask for forgiveness?

Well, before you can expect to be forgiven you need to humbly make an unconditional apology—one that has no buts, no ifs and no excuses. And it shouldn't be a backhanded attempt to get your spouse to apologize. It should sound like this, "I was wrong. Please forgive me." Then follow up with action. You need to show that you've changed and have turned away from your wrong.

Be patient with your mate. They might need some time to see that you're really making the effort.

MY THOUGHTS:

_____

_____

_____

FORGIVENESS-2

What's harder than asking for forgiveness?

Making a decision to give forgiveness is even tougher. Forgiveness is not a feeling. It's a decision. After a matter has been confronted and discussed, and our spouse has asked for forgiveness and changed their ways, we need to decide to grant forgiveness. To make this work, don't bring up the subject again. That means not keeping a record of wrongs. And, don't replay the situation in your mind. If you do, it's like burying the hatchet but keeping the handle uncovered just in case you want to use it again.

Decide to forgive and in time you will forget.

MY THOUGHTS:

_____

_____

_____

MARK BRUNELL—ALL PRO DAD

What does an NFL great know about being a great dad?

He knows a lot. Mark Brunell of the Jacksonville Jaguars is known for being the number five-ranked passer in NFL history. He's also the father of four children. What Brunell brings to quarterbacking he also brings to parenting. In his words, "Being a good quarterback takes determination, dedication and perseverance. Those are also the qualities you need to be a good father."

So, Dads, add those skills to your own fatherhood game plan for a winning relationship with your kids.

MY THOUGHTS:

_____

_____

_____

MR. FIX IT

When you and your spouse disagree, do you try to fix the problem or fix the person?

A Texan was forever pointing out how much bigger and better everything was in his home state. One day he visited a friend in New York who took him to Niagara Falls. Standing near the cascading waterfalls, the New Yorker asked the Texan, "So, do you have anything like this back home?"

Without blinking an eye, the Texan said, "No. But we've got a plumber who can fix it."

Isn't that just like us, trying to fix each other instead of appreciating our differences? Remember, just like Niagara Falls, different can be exciting.

MY THOUGHTS:

_____

_____

_____

LISTEN WITH YOUR EYES

Okay, raise your hand if you've ever told your children, "Look at me when I'm talking to you."

Picture this: you're telling your child something really important. But instead of giving you his full attention, he is half listening and doesn't even stop what he's doing. Doesn't that frustrate you? You've got something important to say, and your child's not listening. Now, stop and think how often we do that to our kids. We keep on cleaning the kitchen, reading the newspaper or watching TV. Sure, we can't always stop what we're doing, but we can try harder.

Let's follow our own advice and look at our children when they're trying to tell us something.

MY THOUGHTS:

_____

_____

_____

THERE IS HOPE

Should you give up hope if your child is having a tough time?

Some of the greatest achievers in history did not have it easy. A research study looked at 400 people including Einstein, Churchill and Freud. It found that three-quarters of them came from troubled childhoods of poverty, broken homes or abuse. Another one-fourth had physical handicaps. If our children fall into these categories we need to focus on their strengths and God-given abilities that can help them overcome the obstacles they face.

Challenges will make our children either strong or weak. It's up to us to give them the encouragement and love to keep their hopes and dreams alive.

MY THOUGHTS:

_____

_____

_____

FAMILY MINUTES

NICKNAMES

Does your family use nicknames?

Nicknames make you feel special. I call my youngest daughter Baby Girl. But I didn't realize how important it is to her until I called her older sister that. That's when my younger daughter said, "No, Daddy, Baby Girl's my name." Nicknames show that you're willing to look at the uniqueness of who someone is. Sometimes it's just a twist on the person's given name: Kim becomes Kimmy or Scott becomes Scotty. Most children love nicknames.

So see your children with new eyes and come up with an affectionate name just for them.

MY THOUGHTS:

CRIS CARTER

There's a new place to turn for marriage advice—the football field.

Retired wide receiver Cris Carter made more than one hundred consecutive starts for the Minnesota Vikings. Even through years of getting targeted, tackled and trampled, no bump or bruise could keep him on the bench. That's the mindset we need for a durable, lasting marriage. You see, if Carter had sat the game out every time he was injured, he would have missed his chance for the good stuff—the diving catch, the 50-yard run or the game-winning touchdown.

So when you feel hurt and discouraged in your marriage—hang tough. The thrill of victory just might be closer than you think.

MY THOUGHTS:

_____

_____

_____

FAMILY MINUTES

GET BOARD

When's the last time you and your kids got "board"?

I don't mean bored as in nothing to do. I mean board as in board games. You don't have to wait for a rainy day or for an evening when the power goes out. Pull them out now. Playing games is obviously a great way to spend time with your kids face to face doing something fun. It also gives you an opportunity to teach them about competition and how to be a good loser and good winner.

So pick up some games like Monopoly, Clue or Scrabble. Then turn off the TV and the computer, and begin the family fun.

MY THOUGHTS:

TOMORROW'S TOO LATE

Tomorrow may be too late.

I recently met a man I'll call Jack. He told me that he hadn't spoken to his grown daughter in three years, and that they'd always had a rocky relationship. Then he got a nice letter from her. Well, weeks passed and Jack still hadn't responded. He thought he needed to strategize. I encouraged him to just be vulnerable and tell her he loves her.

But my last suggestion may have been most important—especially for all of us who have children. I told him to reach out to her today because you never know, tomorrow may be too late.

MY THOUGHTS:

_____

_____

_____

THE PROBLEM WITH DISCIPLINE

Often, the problem with discipline isn't the kids—it's the parents.

Some say their kids just won't behave. But maybe Mom and Dad are just too busy and too tired to deal effectively and lovingly with disciplining their children. Instead, they throw up their hands, look for quick fixes or discipline inconsistently. My wife and I recently decided to cut back on our busyness. We realized that we needed more time and energy to focus on shaping our children's behavior.

Parents, we need to change our behavior before we can expect our kids to change theirs.

MY THOUGHTS:

"MY EYE'S ON YOU" AWARD

Get ready for the "My Eye's on You" award.

One day I got some cardboard, attached some old ribbon to it and held an awards ceremony to honor my kids for doing something good that week. My oldest daughter got the award for joining the church, my younger daughter for doing more than what was expected, and my son for catching a pop fly in baseball. I even gave my wife an award for our twelve years of marriage. The kids acted like it was totally uncool. Yet, that night, all their ribbons were displayed in their rooms.

So keep your eyes on your family, and "catch" them doing something good.

MY THOUGHTS:

COACH DUNGY

Are you too busy to spend time with your kids?

If you answered yes, an NFL head coach wants a few words with you. Although Tony Dungy of the Indianapolis Colts has a demanding schedule, he still makes family the biggest part of his game plan. He takes time to be with his five children—picking them up from school, bringing them to the office. Coach Dungy says fatherhood, not football, is his most important job.

So take a look at your game plan. Strategize time with your kids. Maybe it's taking them to school, maybe it's breakfast. The point is, if an NFL head coach can make time to be a good dad, you can too.

MY THOUGHTS:

BACK TO SCHOOL

Mom and Dad, are you ready for back-to-school time?

As parents, we can follow our children's school progress by looking at their report cards. But how can we measure our performance? When your kids get their grades, review the job you're doing as a parent. Ask your children how else you can help them succeed in the classroom. Do they need more homework help, an earlier bedtime or an extra hug on test days? When children feel supported at home they gain confidence in reading, writing and arithmetic.

So the next time you encourage your kids to do their homework, make sure you're doing yours.

MY THOUGHTS:

CRITICAL THINKING

Are you teaching your children to be critical?

Picture this: the whole family is gathered around the TV and as different people pop onto the screen you make comments about them. "Boy, that guy has some funny hair." Or, "She looks terrible in that jacket." On and on it goes. A little comment here, a little comment there. Well, what you're doing is showing your kids that it's okay to be critical of someone because of the way they look. And at the same time you're putting a lot of value on appearance.

So the next time you have the urge to comment, recall the old adage, "If you don't have something nice to say, don't say anything at all."

MY THOUGHTS:

_____

_____

_____

SUGAR BUSTERS

Are you on a high-protein, low-carb diet such as Sugar Busters, Dr. Atkins or Protein Power?

If you're on the weight-loss wagon—that's fine. But I want to caution you about how your dieting might affect your children. You see, when we focus on appearance, we send the message that looks matter the most. Now, sure, being overweight is unhealthy. But if we obsess about it, our children will too. Studies show that the earlier in life you start dieting, the more likely you are to develop problems with food, leading to serious weight and emotional issues.

So watch your weight. But, more importantly, watch the message you're sending.

MY THOUGHTS:

TO HELP OR NOT TO HELP

If your kids say they don't need help, should you help anyway?

Not too long ago my preteen daughter was rollerblading with some friends. She was having a hard time getting up some steps, so I asked if I could help. She said "No." So, I let her struggle on her own. Later that evening she was upset with me because I didn't help her. You see, she really did want my help but didn't want to admit that in front of her friends.

The lesson: the next time your child refuses your help, consider the circumstances. Put yourself in his or her shoes and be prepared to read between the lines.

MY THOUGHTS:

_____

_____

_____

SHOPPING BATTLES

Have you had a shopping battle with your daughter lately?

You can hear the cry from dressing rooms coast to coast, "Why can't I wear this? Everybody else does!" And most of the time the protester is a preteen or teenage girl who is trying to get her parents to cave in. But don't do it. Hold your ground. Of course, kids just want to fit in, and they see these clothes as harmless. Yet, as adults we know that dressing this way sets our daughters up as sexual objects.

So stand your ground, Mom and Dad. Protect your girls—even if it seems unfashionable.

MY THOUGHTS:

DEFINE YOURSELF

If you had to define yourself, what's the first thing you would say?

Would you talk about your job, your hobbies or your educational background? It's been said, "Out of the fullness of the heart the mouth speaks." That basically means that what you say off the top of your head is usually what's foremost in your heart. Do you define yourself by what you do or by who you are? Maybe you would say you are a committed husband or wife, a loving parent or grandparent.

Take a step back and think about what your answer would be. How do you define yourself?

MY THOUGHTS:

PICKING A FIGHT

Ever felt like picking a fight with your spouse?

You're grouchy. You're ready to unload, and you let the words fly. You take out your frustration on your mate, hoping they'll take the bait. Well, there is a better way to vent. When you see them, just say, "I am cranky." They'll ask why, and that's when you get to let it all out—but more like a report instead of an attack. Your mate can be the comforter and the one who cheers you up.

There are two positive outcomes from this approach. You'll still get to vent but without the damaging consequences of a full-blown fight.

MY THOUGHTS:

_____

_____

_____

BACK-TO-SCHOOL BOOST

Are you ready to give your kids a back-to-school boost?

The start of a new school year can be scary for children. They're in new classes, with new teachers and often new classmates. So as a parent, this is a time it's especially important to stay connected to your kids. Try to make sure you're home when they get home. If you work, make a point of calling them as soon as you know they're in. Then, when you do get to see them, spend some extra time talking about their day and how things are going.

Be perceptive. Show your children you're ready to listen and give a back-to-school boost.

MY THOUGHTS:

FOOTBALL SEASON

Hey, Dad, are you planning on watching some football this season?

What a great way to spend a weekend afternoon. Settle into the couch, grab some nachos and let the games begin. Pretty soon you've spent hours glued to the tube. Nothing wrong with that—I'll be doing it too. But we need to give our children equal time. For every game you watch, plan on doing something fun with your kids. Grab your own football and head outside to play catch or go to the library together.

By all means, enjoy the game. But make sure your kids aren't stuck riding the bench.

MY THOUGHTS:

PREGNANT WIVES

Do you know what your pregnant wife wants to hear?

First, let me tell you what she doesn't want to hear. "Wow! You're getting big. What happened to the fun woman I married?" Or, "Why don't you ever cook anymore?" Guys, pregnancy is a physically and emotionally draining experience, and your wife needs your support and understanding. So be patient and realize how she's feeling.

Oh, and what should you say? Try, "Honey, I'll get dinner. Don't worry, I know you're just tired." And of course, "I love you" is always appreciated.

MY THOUGHTS:

TEENS—REAL WORLD

Is your teenager ready for the real world?

There will come a time when your teen will be on their own whether it's at college or taking a job and moving out. Is he or she ready? Every teen should know the basics: how to do laundry (whites and colors), cook a simple meal and handle their finances. If they haven't learned, give them a crash course in living in the real world. Show them how to do the laundry. Teach them how to make a few simple, healthy meals. And explain how to do a straightforward budget.

These are some of the basics they'll need in the real world.

MY THOUGHTS:

DAUNTE CULPEPPER

It takes a remarkable person to adopt a child.

Emma Culpepper, now in her late-eighties, adopted fifteen children over her lifetime. More than twenty years ago, she adopted a 1-day-old boy who had been born in prison. Emma raised this boy with love and discipline. He went on to set football records at the University of Central Florida and is now the quarterback of the Minnesota Vikings. Daunte Culpepper is living out his dream because of the sacrifice and love of a woman named Emma.

She had the compassion and heart to give a little baby born in prison a future full of hope.

MY THOUGHTS:

GO FISHING

Are you looking for something fun to do with your kids?

I love taking my kids fishing. It can be a wonderful adventure. And even if you're not an experienced angler, you can still make it an outing to remember. To start with, if you don't have your own fishing rods or tackle, rent or borrow some. Then head to the lake, creek or pond. The goal is to spend time together. Create a shared memory and talk without the distraction of TV or video games.

And, hey, just putting that slimy bait on the hook will give you lots to talk about. So get together and...go fish!

MY THOUGHTS:

_____

_____

_____

241   August 29

FAMILY MINUTES

STOP, DROP AND LISTEN

Tired of getting bombarded at the door when you get home?

Try the stop, drop, and listen method. I know, when you get in from work you just want some time to yourself. But trust me on this. If you give your kids time up front, just a few minutes will satisfy them. It works like this. Stop right when you walk in the door. Drop to your knees and get at eye level with your children. Then, listen. Let them tell you about their day. In a matter of minutes they'll be ready to move on from you to something else.

So stop, drop, and listen. Then you can have that relaxing moment you've been waiting for.

MY THOUGHTS:

_____

_____

_____

Kids and Culture

SCARY STATISTICS

Want to hear something scary?

If you think pornography is harmless, you should read on. In a study where researchers interviewed serial killers, they found that most of the killers had been exposed to pornography before they even hit puberty. You see, those early images desensitized them. Eventually the make-believe world of pornography wasn't enough, and they went on to rape and murder. Now, you may be thinking, "Thank goodness my kids have never seen pornography." But have they seen sexually explicit movies or TV programs?

Pornography is out there. And it's up to us to shield our children from its dangers.

MY THOUGHTS:

_____

_____

_____

PERFECT PARENTS

Have you ever met a perfect parent?

While no parent is perfect, sometimes we act like we are. Here's an example: our child accidentally knocks over a glass of milk. If we happen to be tired and edgy, we might say, "Do you always have to spill your milk?" Of course later we realize we were out of line. But we're afraid that if we admit our mistake, our kids won't respect our authority. Guess what? The opposite is true. It's tough to admit we're wrong. But by apologizing we show our kids that it's more important to be fair and just than to be right.

And consider this: admitting our mistakes also shows that you don't have to be a perfect parent or a perfect person.

MY THOUGHTS:

_____

_____

_____

TENSION AT HOME

Okay, I admit that I blew it again.

I came home the other night, and I was in a bad mood. But instead of just saying, "I'm cranky," I huffed and puffed all evening. Well, my wife was tired herself so she had little patience for my mood. We went back and forth with sarcastic remarks and little digs until bedtime. Then, my daughter brought me back to reality when she said, "Daddy, when you and Mom act that way it makes me sad and angry."

First, I apologized. Then I told her we shouldn't talk to each other like that and promised I'd try to do better. And I will.

MY THOUGHTS:

REALITY CHECK

Do your children need a reality check?

There's no way around it. Our society is materialistic. So, kids can easily think it's the norm to have hundred dollar Nikes or back-to-school clothes from Saks Fifth Avenue. Perhaps we need to introduce our children to the real world. We can take them to volunteer at a soup kitchen or a homeless shelter. Or how about sending them on a mission trip to a place where poverty means going to bed hungry instead of going without a TV in every room?

Experiences like these can help them see the reality of what most of the world is really all about.

MY THOUGHTS:

_____

_____

_____

WORLD ON THEIR SHOULDERS

Here's a question for you: how much does the world weigh?

Well, if you really want to know, ask a single parent. Of course the point of that riddle is that single parents often feel like they have the whole world on their shoulders. So how can we help them out when our own lives are incredibly busy? Just start with the little things. The next time you're washing your car, offer to wash their car too. Drop off dinner or volunteer to take their children for the evening so they can get a little time to themselves.

Being a parent is a big job. But being a single parent is an even bigger one. So lighten their load and help take the world off their shoulders.

MY THOUGHTS:

TEENS' TEACHERS

When's the last time you talked to your teenager's teachers?

By the time kids reach middle or high school, parent-teacher conferences are the exception, not the rule. So to stay on top of how your teen is doing in the classroom, talk with his or her teachers. It will take some planning since most kids have several instructors by the time they hit middle school. But the effort will be worth it. Both the teacher and your teen will see you're taking an active role. You'll also have a better chance of finding out about classroom challenges before they become classroom problems.

Finally, get to know who's teaching your teen because it may be someone who really ends up having an influence on their life.

MY THOUGHTS:

GRANDPARENT'S DAY

Think about this picture of loneliness.

It's a grandparent, sitting alone, hoping day after day to hear from his or her grandchildren. Well, this Sunday is Grandparent's Day. So why not make a point of calling or stopping by to see your grandparents? If you don't have a close relationship, this could be a way to try to lay the foundation for one. Unfortunately, none of my grandparents are living. So if yours are, take advantage of a blessing that many of us don't have.

Reach out to those who sit in loneliness—longing to hear the voice or see the face of their grandchildren.

MY THOUGHTS:

FAMILY MINUTES

TRAVIS HALL

What comes to mind when you watch NFL football—intensity, toughness, forcefulness?

Those images describe Atlanta Falcons defensive tackle Travis Hall in action. He's definitely an NFL tough guy, and he says the key to being a good defensive player is having the right strategy. According to Hall, you have to be prepared to face any and all circumstances. And when he's off the football field, he applies that same principle to being a good dad.

But being prepared doesn't just happen—in football or in parenting. Just like becoming a successful NFL player, becoming a good father takes time, dedication and perseverance.

MY THOUGHTS:

_____

_____

_____

JUST SAY IT!

A picture might be worth a thousand words, but the right words are priceless.

Do you want to witness the power of words in action? Then do this. The next time you see your wife lay a heavy compliment on her. What's a heavy compliment? Well, if you rarely say kind things, even a "Hey, whatever you're cooking sure smells good," can go a long way. The point is, make it your business to understand what's important to your wife and compliment her on it. If she's passionate about her work in the office or at home, take notice of something she's done recently.

Just say it! You might be surprised what she says back.

MY THOUGHTS:

FAMILY MINUTES

SIBLING CONFLICTS

Ever feel like a referee in a boxing match?

I was visiting with a friend the other day who has three teen boys. She said they don't get into fights. Wow! I can't relate to that. My mom and dad did a good job encouraging me and my two brothers to love one another, and we're best friends today. Yet, we still had brotherly brawls and beat each other up on a few occasions when we were teens.

Now I'm not advocating that, but sibling conflicts can occur. So try not to get down about it. Just keep telling and teaching them to honor one another with words and actions.

MY THOUGHTS:

_____

_____

_____

SECURITY SYSTEM

Want to know what the number one source of security is for children?

Knowing their parents love each other and are committed to making their marriage work—for life—gives kids more security than anything else. Living in a world where over half of marriages break up, our kids know what's going on. They hear about divorce from friends whose parents are splitting up, and it's only natural that they should wonder about their own parents. Children need a stable environment—they need reassurance.

They want to know that Mom and Dad are committed for the long haul, and that when they said "'til death do us part" they meant it.

MY THOUGHTS:

ALLPRODAD.COM

Do you know what it takes to be an All Pro Dad?

The head coach of the Indianapolis Colts, Tony Dungy, says it takes compassion and commitment. He should know. He's the father of five and the head coach of the All Pro Dad team. All Pro Dad is a free resource for fathers. It gives them the equipment they need to move from the sidelines to the starting lineup.

So to hear parenting wisdom from the All Pro Dad team click on over to our website Allprodad.com. You'll hear from NFL greats like Mark Brunell, Steve Largent and Trent Dilfer.

Get ready to join the team because you can be an All Pro Dad too.

MY THOUGHTS:

_____

_____

_____

Fatherhood

BREAKFAST SURPRISE

Having a hard time getting your kids out of bed and out the door on time? See if this sounds familiar. The alarm goes off. "Time to get up," you tell your kids.

Ten minutes later, they're still in bed saying, "I'm tired. I don't want to go to school."

Maybe they need an incentive. At my house, it's a weekly surprise breakfast—chocolate chip pancakes, cheese eggs, you name it. If my kids are downstairs at the appointed time, they get to dig in. If they're not, they get a less exciting meal. The key is, don't tell them which morning is the morning. That way, they'll be on time, just in case it's the day.

So to get them out of bed, get out the griddle.

MY THOUGHTS:

_____

_____

_____

FAMILY MINUTES

DATING AWARENESS

Would you let your daughter go off with a complete stranger?

"Of course not!" you say. Well, think about how some teens date. Your daughter gets a call, and the next thing you know, some guy is honking the horn and waiting in his car. Now, consider that stranger example again. When you send your child off on a date with someone you don't know, it's the same thing. So make sure you know who your daughter or son is spending time with. Try to meet the other kid's parents. Invite him or her to spend time with your family at home before the date.

Be aware of what's going on in your child's dating life.

MY THOUGHTS:

_____

_____

_____

ANGER AND ARGUMENTS

You've heard it said, "I was so angry I couldn't see straight."

Well, there's some truth to that statement. When we're angry, our adrenaline starts pumping and our body automatically goes into survival mode. It's like being chased by a big bear. And when that happens our physical strength increases but our brain's ability to concentrate and reason decreases. In a state of anger or rage you cannot think rationally.

So the next time you're angry with your spouse, wait until your adrenaline stops pumping. Then, try to resolve the problem when you can really think it through.

MY THOUGHTS:

FAMILY MINUTES

GOALSGUY.COM

Are you helping your kids plan for their future?

One great way to help them chart a course is to help them set goals. Without goals, it's easy to just drift along. In fact, an old proverb says, "...without vision, the people perish." To help your children create a vision for their future, visit the website goalsguy.com. The site has guidelines for creating goals and ideas for tracking their progress. It talks about how setting and reaching goals can build confidence in your kids.

So encourage them to set their sights on the future—one goal at a time.

MY THOUGHTS:

FORGIVENESS

When should you say you're sorry, and when should you ask for forgiveness?

Think they're the same thing? Well, not really. My wife and I are trying to teach our kids the difference. Sorry is okay for accidents, like spilling milk or bumping into someone. But when our kids do something on purpose—calling their brother or sister a name, not sharing—then they have to say, "I was wrong. Please forgive me." And they have to do it without making excuses.

Asking for forgiveness is an experience that teaches humility and responsibility.

MY THOUGHTS:

September 16

MARRIAGE LICENSE

Have you ever heard of divorce before marriage?

Some friends of mine went to get their marriage license, and the clerk of the court gave them a little booklet. It was supposed to be about marriage, yet most if it discussed the ins and outs of divorce. Well, if our marriages are going to last, we need a mindset of permanence, a decision to make marriage work. My friends threw that little booklet out because for them divorce is not an option.

They trashed the dos and don'ts of divorce and are staying true to their commitment to each other—for life.

MY THOUGHTS:

_____

_____

_____

PARENTING HELP

"No! And you can't make me!"

That's basically what a 6-year-old told her mom when asked to clean her room. The girl stomped away, fell to the floor and cried. Then the mom who told us about this got so mad she went to her room and hid!

So what's a parent to do? Set up a chore chart with rewards and consequences. If your kids clean their rooms and do their other weekly chores they get a reward—like an allowance. If not, the consequence is no allowance. And if they cry, don't give in. Calmly remind them that if they do their chores, they'll get their rewards.

Remember, children need to learn life is full of rewards and consequences.

MY THOUGHTS:

FAMILY MINUTES

KNOWING YOUR STRENGTH

Parents, do you really know your own strength?

If you watch a weight lifter work out, you'll notice something—it takes more effort to pull the weight up than to let it down. But the effort is worth it because pulling up builds muscles. That's a good principle to keep in mind as we raise our children. Booker T. Washington, the great educator, said there are two ways of exerting strength. One is pushing down, the other is pulling up. How do you exert your strength, your authority, over your children? Do you push down with criticism or pull up with praise?

Sure, it takes more effort to pull than to push, but you'll build a stronger and healthier child in the process.

MY THOUGHTS:

_____

_____

_____

PRAYER POWER

Here's something simple that could be a boost for your golden years.

A report from Duke University says that senior citizens who pray "may add years to their lives." That's right. The people in the study who had regular prayer, meditation or Bible study lived longer than those who didn't. Even when they prayed as little as once a month, it made a big difference. Both prayer and meditation have been proven to reduce stress. And reducing stress strengthens your immune system, helping to keep up a good defense against diseases.

So give it a try. Pray your way toward better health and a longer life.

MY THOUGHTS:

FAMILY MINUTES

REMOTE CONTROL

The new fall TV shows are here, and the battle for the remote begins.

Not everything on TV will please both you and your kids. But there's a way to avoid the fight over what they can and can't watch. Before you even turn on the television, create a *Family TV Guide* and list the programs you and your children agree are acceptable. If there's a show they really want to watch but you have your doubts, watch it together. And while you may not like what you see, afterward you can discuss the issues the program raises.

Help your kids learn to discern between good and bad programming, and give the remote a rest.

MY THOUGHTS:

_____

_____

_____

FAMILY TIME CHALLENGE

If you are willing to do whatever it takes to help your child succeed in life, then I have a challenge for you.

Commit to spend one hour of one week, one-on-one, with each of your children. That's the first step in the Family Time Challenge. The Challenge, however, is just a starting point. Hopefully, after taking it, you'll set aside one-on-one time every week. Choose an activity that allows for talking, doing and relating. Studies show that children who have parents do better in school and are less likely to turn to crime. So choose your week, set your hour, and take the Family Time Challenge.

Not only will your children benefit from time together, but so will you.

MY THOUGHTS:

_____

_____

_____

September 22

DATING 101

Dads, do you know how to teach Dating 101?

Well, here's the basic course description: your son is going to learn how to treat women by watching you. That's right. Do you hold the door open for women as you enter a building? Do you get the car door for your wife? That's just the beginning of Dating 101. For an intensive course, take your wife out for dinner and take your son along. Point out along the way the things you're doing to make your "date" feel special. Then have your wife talk about why manners and politeness are important.

Dating 101. Dads, in this course you're the professor.

MY THOUGHTS:

FAMILY DAY

How can family dinners help keep your kids drug-free?

The National Center on Addiction and Substance Abuse at Columbia University, or CASA, found that having regular family dinners can actually help your kids resist drugs. It also discovered that children who eat dinner with their families only twice a week or less are more likely to smoke cigarettes and marijuana and drink alcohol. So CASA has made today Family Day to remind you how important it is to eat dinner together.

So pull up a chair for the sake of your kids.

MY THOUGHTS:

I BLEW IT—AGAIN

"I'm late for an appointment, I've got to go."

Those were my words to my young daughter as I ran out the door. Of course just a few minutes before that, I had promised to help her with her piano lessons. Later my wife called and said, "Didn't you see your little girl in tears running after you asking for your help?" Well, my heart sank. That night I went to my daughter and asked her to forgive me. I told her how bad I felt, and she accepted my apology.

Dads, when you blow it like I did, ask your child for forgiveness. Your humility will create a bond with your child that will grow and grow.

MY THOUGHTS:

_____

_____

_____

PARENTS AND SMOKING

Want to keep your kids from smoking?

A study found that what parents say to their kids about smoking cigarettes has more of an influence on them than peer pressure. Children who have parents who are very clear and stern about not wanting them to smoke are less likely to, while kids whose parents are more accepting of smoking are much more likely to light up. This study out of Dartmouth says that even parents who smoke can influence their children not to, as long as they tell their kids they're dead set against it.

So take a firm stand against smoking.

MY THOUGHTS:

BEETHOVEN

If you are you often at a loss for words when someone you know is hurting, then, instead of trying to find the right words, use your heart.

The composer Ludwig van Beethoven was not known for his social graces. And because of his deafness, he found conversation difficult. But when a close friend's son died, Beethoven, overcome with sorrow, rushed to his friend's house. While he couldn't say how he felt, he did see a piano, and for the next half-hour poured out his grief through the keyboard. No one else's support meant so much to his friend.

While none of us can play like Beethoven, we can follow his example and give from the heart. So if you're ever stumped for the right words to say, just give the best you have to offer—yourself.

MY THOUGHTS:

UNEMPLOYMENT

If unemployment hits you, are you prepared?

I don't mean financially. I mean, do you know how to help your kids handle the trauma? First, talk to them. Young children can think job loss is somehow their fault. They might even feel guilty about needing things that require you to spend money. And try to keep up your family's normal routines. Although it's easy to pull away from people in stressful times, your children need the familiar. Finally, reassure them with extra love and attention.

Remember, even when your job situation is shaky, your home life doesn't have to be.

MY THOUGHTS:

WHAT MAKES A GOOD MARRIAGE?

What makes a good marriage?

Ask most people this question and you'll probably hear something about love. But in their book, *When Bad Things Happen to Good Marriages*, Drs. Les and Leslie Parrot go through extensive research and find that a "good marriage is built by two peoples' capacity to adjust to bad things." And they say, there are five tools every good marriage uses to battle bad things: ownership, hope, empathy, forgiveness and commitment.

If you are willing to not only learn about these tools, but then use them properly, you will be able to start building something really good.

MY THOUGHTS:

BEGIN AND END THE DAY RIGHT

"Get out of bed—you're late!"

Is that the way the day kicks off around your house? Well, if so, tomorrow try to start and end your children's day in a positive way. Think of it as matching bookends. Wake them up gently. Greet them with a smile, a hug or a kiss. Tell them you love them. Then, end the day gently too. Be there for your kids at bedtime, when the day comes to a close. Be loving and comforting—rub their backs, read to them, tuck them in and pray with them.

Give your kids' day positive bookends, and the hours in between are bound to go better.

MY THOUGHTS:

_____

_____

_____

PUSHING FOR PERFECTION

Are you pushing your kids to perfection?

With this new school year are you already expecting too much from your kids? Yes, it's okay to want your children to do their best. But when their best ends up earning a B instead of an A, are you willing to accept it? How about if they really try their hardest and get a C?

To help our children reach their potential, we need to give them the tools to succeed. That might include tutoring or extra study time. But it also includes being loving and supportive, even when their abilities don't meet our expectations.

MY THOUGHTS:

_____

_____

_____

THE SCARED LITTLE GIRL

Do you wish you could stand up to your fears?

There was once a young girl from a poverty-stricken, broken home. She dreamed of being a performer, but she was terribly shy and had awful attacks of stage fright. Well, she decided that nothing would stand in the way of her dream. She accepted the fact that she was scared and went out on that stage anyway. You see, she realized that she didn't have to get rid of her fears but just had to move forward in spite of them.

Today you know that little girl who followed her dream as Carol Burnett.

MY THOUGHTS:

ADVICE GIVER

Are you a listener or an advice giver?

Tell me if this sounds familiar: your wife or your husband comes to the door feeling sad and discouraged. "What's wrong?" you ask. They tell you how hard their job is and how mean their boss is. So you say, "Hey, hit the problem head on. Talk to your boss about it if you're having a hard time." Now, that sounds like a fair response, but it actually invalidates their feelings. Instead, try empathizing, "I am so sorry you had a bad day. That must be awful to work for someone like that."

Listen first. Then, if they ask for advice, feel free to give it.

MY THOUGHTS:

BIG IDEAS FROM LITTLE PLACES

Do you listen when your children have something to say?

Big ideas can come from little places. One hundred and forty years ago in Maine, a boy named Hanson Gregory was watching his mother cook fried dough. He noticed how the middle of the pastry stayed mushy and uncooked. "Mom," he said, "why not cut a hole in the dough before you fry it?" Well, because Hanson's mother listened to her son, today we enjoy the doughnut.

So pay attention when your children offer their suggestions because the world's next great idea just might be in your own home.

MY THOUGHTS:

_____

_____

_____

HEAT OF THE MOMENT

Do you discipline your kids in the heat of the moment?

It's tough to think clearly when you're angry and agitated. Before you know it, you've said the wrong thing. You can overreact—"You're grounded until you finish high school!" Or, you can get mean, "Can't you do anything right?" Either way, disciplining like that probably won't be very effective. So the next time your kids do something that requires discipline, step back and cool off.

Wait until the heat of the moment has passed. Then, review your established consequences and calmly pass them on to your children.

MY THOUGHTS:

PRETEEN DAUGHTERS

Do you know what your preteen daughter needs?

She needs you, Dad! When she's going through hormonal and physical changes, she needs you to tell her she's pretty, especially if she has acne or is uncomfortable with her appearance. She needs you to give her affection, even though it may seem awkward to her and to you. And she needs you to show her unconditional love. Let her know that you love her no matter what she does.

In short, she needs to know that she is a young lady with infinite value, dignity and worth.

MY THOUGHTS:

MARRIAGE TURBULENCE

Experiencing turbulence in your marriage?

From my experience as a private pilot, I can tell you that bad weather and air turbulence are just a part of flying. While some turbulence can be avoided, sometimes you have to fly through it. Building an intimate marriage is similar to flying a plane. Sure, most of us would like to avoid turbulence in our marriage. Still, there are times you just have to fly through it.

The key to navigating through it is to learn to resolve conflict and communicate with each other in a way that turns marital turbulence into a smooth flight.

MY THOUGHTS:

_____

_____

_____

FAILURE AS A FATHER?

Ever feel like a failure as a father?

Well, you're not alone. I've met with hundreds of fathers who feel that way, including me. Whether your children are 15 or 45 years old, it's never too late to talk, call or visit them. Be willing to admit your failures and shortcomings and then commit to work on becoming the kind of father they need you to be.

And if you go to our website, AllProDad.com, you'll find some free tools to help you build or reconstruct your relationship—the kind of relationship both you and your children have been longing for.

MY THOUGHTS:

WORDS OF HOPE

See if you can guess who wrote the following words.

"Life is a dream, realize it. Life is a challenge, meet it. Life is a duty, complete it. Life is a promise, fulfill it. Life is a song, sing it. Life is a struggle, accept it. Life is life, fight for it." Do you have any idea? Well, the author was someone who suffered more than most of us ever will. Yet, she found joy. She kept hoping. She kept giving. If she could have that attitude, we should too.

So who wrote those words? Mother Teresa.

MY THOUGHTS:

BREAST CANCER

Do you have the facts on breast cancer?

October is breast cancer awareness month. Experts say the key to surviving breast cancer is early detection. In fact, 95 percent of women whose cancer is detected early have a 5-year survival rate. Early detection methods include monthly self-examinations and mammograms. As a general rule, women should get annual mammogram screenings starting at age 40. But talk to your doctor in case you should start earlier.

Get the facts on breast cancer to help you or someone you love beat this disease.

MY THOUGHTS:

HO-HO-NO

Can you believe some stores already have Christmas displays out?

Well, since they're getting ready, shouldn't you? I don't mean start decorating your Christmas tree. But now is a good time to decide on a gift list and how much you'll spend. The holidays can be wonderful. However, too many financial pressures can steal a lot of the joy from the season. So talk to your spouse, your children, and your extended family—they might be feeling the same way. Set a dollar limit on gifts and draw names instead of exchanging presents with everyone. Can you cook? Bake someone's favorite treat. Or, let your kids make gifts for the entire family.

Once you get rid of the money pressures, you can really get into the holiday spirit.

MY THOUGHTS:

_____

_____

_____

EYE TO EYE

How about better communication with your kids in two easy steps?

It may sound like a gimmick—but it works. Are you tired of repeating yourself over and over to your kids? Well, try this. Step one—stand or sit at eye level with your child. Then start talking. If he looks away or steals a glance at the TV, start over. Step two—echo. Let him repeat what you've said. That way you know he got the message. It works like this: "Billy, please clean your room."

"Yes, Daddy."

Now here's where the echo comes in. "So what are you going to do, Billy?"

"I'm going to clean my room."

Eye level and echo—a two-step communication plan that really works.

MY THOUGHTS:

WHY?

Do you look down on single parents?

Well, remember, single parents come from all circumstances. Some were widowed. Some were left by their spouse. Some had their children outside of marriage. But no matter how they got there, their job is the same—to raise their children the best they know how. And regardless of how you feel about single parents, there's a big reason they need our support—their children.

More than 30 percent of American children are now being raised by a single parent. They are the innocent bystanders in these homes. So we need to stop judging and start helping.

MY THOUGHTS:

CONTAGIOUS

I want to warn you about something that's very contagious.

On an episode of "Touched by an Angel," a woman almost committed suicide because the angel Monica somehow caught and passed on a damaging human virus—a bad attitude. You see, Monica's sour attitude moved from person to person until it reached that vulnerable lady. We might think our angry tone or impatient sarcasm won't cause any damage. But what if the person you encounter is at the end of their rope? Your grouchiness could push them over the edge.

So, instead of starting a bad attitude outbreak, don't forget that a good attitude is just as contagious.

MY THOUGHTS:

FAMILY MINUTES

SIX A's OF GOOD PARENTING

Do you know the six A's of good parenting?

Youth expert Josh McDowell says the key to good parenting is staying connected to your kids. And, he says, to do that you need the six A's. The first is affirmation, which means acknowledging the child's feelings. The second A is acceptance. Let your kids know you love them not because of what they achieve, but because of who they are.

Appreciation is the next A. Catch your kids doing something right and express your appreciation to them. The fourth A is availability. When you're available to your children, you're showing them that they're important. Next is affection. Our kids feel lovable when we are affectionate toward them. The final A is accountability. When we hold our children accountable it gives them a sense of responsibility and self-control.

So strive to make the grade when it comes to the six A's of good parenting: affirmation, acceptance, appreciation, availability, affection and accountability.

MY THOUGHTS:

WORD POWER

If you're having a tough time in your marriage, let me give you some encouraging words.

One of the ways we strengthen the bond with our spouse is good communication. And that means choosing our words carefully and using a positive tone of voice. A proverb says, "Reckless words pierce like a sword, but the tongue of the wise brings healing." I'll admit it. I've been reckless so many times while talking to my wife—mean words, condescending tones and critical looks.

Bring words of healing, not hurting, into your marriage. You may even have to bite your tongue to do it.

MY THOUGHTS:

_____

_____

_____

FAMILY MINUTES

DECISIONS...DECISIONS

Here's another reason to put limits on your kids' TV time.

You've heard the experts say it, and now kids agree: violence on TV encourages youth violence. More than half of the teenagers interviewed in Family First's *Kids and Violence Survey* point the finger at violence in the media. So, as parents, do we just lay down the law? I don't think so. Our children should be part of the decision-making process. When my 9-year-old daughter wants to watch a TV program, I ask her, "Do you think we should watch this?"

I want her to learn to discern, so she'll have the tools for making wise decisions on her own.

MY THOUGHTS:

MOMMY BOOM

First we had the baby boom, now we have the mommy boom.

A trend has caught the eye of researchers. More and more women are giving up their paychecks to be stay-at-home moms. A national study found that a majority of parents feel their kids are better off when one parent stays home. That belief is prompting some drastic changes.

One mom told *USA Today* that she and her husband sold the house they were living in so she could be a stay-at-home mom. Why? "I would call to check in," she said, "and I'd hear the baby crying. My heart would just break."

MY THOUGHTS:

_____

_____

_____

DISCIPLINING WITH YOUR EX

So, you want to make things miserable for your ex?

You've decided you won't agree with him or her on anything, including disciplining your children. Sure, you might succeed in raising your ex's blood pressure, but the real target of your efforts will actually be your own flesh and blood—your kids. They will only become confused and frustrated by the mixed signals from you and your former spouse. Instead, do what's in your kids' best interest. Sit down as grown adults and agree on how you will raise and discipline them.

Work with your ex so you won't end up making your children's lives miserable.

MY THOUGHTS:

_____

_____

_____

PERFECT TIMING

You've heard it before—there's no time like the present.

As the holidays approach, we often start making plans to visit family. And once we get there, we'll probably see someone we haven't seen in a while. That person may have meant a lot to us in our younger years.

So why not make up your mind right now to have something special to say when you see them. Instead of making small talk, tell them thanks for making a difference in your life. Instead of just thinking a loving thought—share it. Instead of slapping your dad on the back when you get home, give him a hug and say, "I love you, Dad."

There really is no time like the present.

MY THOUGHTS:

_____

_____

_____

THEY'LL DO WHAT WE DO

No matter what you do for a living, there's one job that all fathers share—being a role model for their children.

Even if you don't want to be—you are. For example, when you get angry in traffic you have the opportunity to model self-restraint. When you get too much change back at the grocery store, there's your chance to model honesty. And when you wrongly accuse your son or daughter of something, that's the perfect time to admit your mistake and teach them about humility.

It all boils down to the fact that children may not always listen to what we say, but they almost always do what we do.

MY THOUGHTS:

COSMO GIRLS

Parents, is your teenage daughter a Cosmo girl?

Teen girls are bombarded with fashion magazines. From *Teen* to *YM* to *Cosmo Girl*, these publications not only give advice on hair and make-up but also on questionable topics. So what's a parent to do? Read the magazine to determine if the content is appropriate for your daughter. Discuss with her the difference between beauty consciousness and beauty obsession. And use the subject of sexuality from articles and advertisements to talk with her about boundaries.

Remember, being herself is more important for your daughter than being a Cosmo girl.

MY THOUGHTS:

FAMILY MINUTES

BUILDING CONFIDENCE IN YOUR KIDS

How do you build confidence in your kids?

A friend of mine has a 6-foot-tall daughter who asked him to take her to the prom. Since she wanted to wear spiked heels, he was the only one tall enough to take her. She wasn't concerned about what others thought. You see, she followed her heart, not her friends. And she was able to do that because her father had instilled confidence in her by letting her know that she was a unique and beautiful individual.

So let your daughter know that she is special, one of a kind. She may not ask you to the prom, but she'll go with confidence.

MY THOUGHTS:

POSITIVE CHANGE

Can you go twenty-four hours without saying something negative?

Well, can you? Try to go through one day without saying anything mean, catty or negative. That means that every word that comes out of your mouth should be free from sarcasm, bitterness and accusations. The test applies to everything you say to your husband, your wife, your children, your co-workers...and even what you say about your boss when he or she is not around.

So try it for a day. If people are shocked at the "new you," then maybe you really have been too negative, and it is time for a change.

MY THOUGHTS:

FAMILY MINUTES

LISTENING TO YOUR TEEN

Are you really listening to your teenager?

There are three things you can do to make sure you're connecting with your teen during those tough years. First, give them your full attention. That means you must stop what you're doing—whether it's sweeping the floor or flipping through a magazine. Make eye contact and turn toward him or her. Second, watch their body language. Are they tense, anxious or sad? Finally, be an active part of the conversation. Rephrase what they have said and repeat it back to them so you know you got it right.

If you really listen to your teen, they will know that you really care.

MY THOUGHTS:

_____

_____

_____

ONE-MINUTE BOOST

Want to give your marriage a boost in just sixty seconds?

Leave your spouse a sweet note. That's right—a note. You'll be amazed at the power of the pen. If you head out of the house first, leave it on their car. Or, hide a note where you know they'll find it. A friend of mine used the letters from a half-finished scrabble game to create a surprise note for his wife. Another husband leaves his wife and young son a note every morning. Sometimes it's just a few words on a napkin or a cereal box top.

So, while it only takes a minute to write a few encouraging words, the boost it gives may last all day long.

MY THOUGHTS:

_____

_____

_____

DAY OF REST

If you're feeling worn out, I could have just what you need.

Does this sound like your life? Monday—work, grocery shop, carpool to soccer practice. Tuesday—work, kids to the dentist, yard work. You get the picture. It's obvious that somewhere in there you need a day of rest. "Impossible," you say. You're just too busy? Well, here's the plan. Make Sunday your day of rest. Ancient cultures and some present-day religions still practice this. And research shows that one day of rest makes you more effective for the other six.

So this Sunday, ignore the lawn mower, steer clear of errands and plan for a day of rest.

MY THOUGHTS:

_____

_____

FAMILY MINUTES

SHAPE THE FUTURE

Ever wish you could shape the future?

Well, you can. And you don't even need to hop on a time machine because your very own link to tomorrow is closer than you think. In fact, it's right in your own home—your children. How you raise your kids today will affect your family's quality of life in the years and generations to come. If you nurture, love and discipline them now, your tomorrows will be stable and secure. Neglect their needs and you'll find a future of heartache and dysfunction. A wise person once said it's easier to raise children than fix adults.

So start shaping tomorrow today, and make sure your mark on the future is a positive one.

MY THOUGHTS:

_____

_____

_____

WINSTON CHURCHILL

Today's parenting advice comes from Winston Churchill.

On October 29, 1941, Britain had been at war with Germany for over two years. It was a dark time for this proud nation. Yet, it was on that day Churchill delivered his famous speech saying, "Never give in, never give in, never, never, never." Well, as a mom or dad it may be your darkest hour. You just caught your child with drugs. Your teenage daughter just told you she's pregnant. Your son is sitting in jail. Now is definitely not the time to surrender. This is the time your child needs your strength and encouragement more than ever.

They need you to fight for them. Never give in. Never give up.

MY THOUGHTS:

LOSE THE LECTURE

Are most of the conversations you have with your teen lectures?

The next time you and your teenager get into a discussion, try this—listen. Teenagers want to be heard, but most often parents want to give advice. Yet, once a child reaches the teenage years, he wants to figure things out for himself. So help him in a more subtle way. Start by listening. Then, instead of lecturing, share some of your own experiences of how you handled your teen years. Be honest. Kids appreciate it when adults own up to their mistakes.

And, who knows, maybe if they hear ours, they won't make the same ones.

MY THOUGHTS:

_____

_____

_____

STEPPARENTING DISCIPLINE

How does a stepparent discipline?

There is only one answer—very carefully. Experts say that in the beginning of a step-parenting relationship, the disciplining should be left to the biological parent. While the stepparent can be involved in deciding on rules and consequences, the biological parent should do the actual enforcing. Meanwhile, there are other ways the stepparent can develop a relationship with the children—show affection, share values and set limits.

So concentrate on laying a good foundation and wait until the time is right for you to share in the disciplining.

MY THOUGHTS:

MIND READER

Do you expect your spouse to be a mind reader?

Maybe you're not the type to go around telling your husband or wife that you love them. They should know how you feel, right? Plus, it might not come naturally to you. But sometimes it's nice to hear those three little words. So this holiday season if you get your spouse a card—that's great. And if you decide to get them a gift—that's great too. But make a point of voicing your feelings. Actually say, "I love you."

Not only may you make their holiday season really special, but you'll give them a break from being a mind reader.

MY THOUGHTS:

STAND UP AND BE COUNTED

It's time to stand up and be counted.

My wife, Susan, saw some kids in the neighborhood who did not look familiar: two young boys each on a bike dragging another bike behind them. She caught up with them in her car and yelled to them to drop the bike, and they did. She stopped the thieves in action.

Now, I'm not suggesting that you endanger yourself or your family. But we do need to stand up and stand strong against crime and violence in our neighborhoods for both our families' and our children's sake.

MY THOUGHTS:

_____

_____

_____

ONE VOTE

Will your vote really make a difference?

Consider this: In 1776 one vote gave America the English language instead of German. In 1868 one vote saved President Andrew Johnson from impeachment. In 1923 one vote gave Adolf Hitler leadership of the Nazi Party. In 1960 Richard Nixon lost the presidential election to John F. Kennedy by a margin of less than one vote per precinct. And according to the Federal Election Commission, the 2000 presidential election was won by only 537 votes in the state of Florida.

So will your vote make a difference? The best way to find out is to cast it in the first place.

MY THOUGHTS:

_____

_____

_____

FAMILY MINUTES

HABIT FORMING

Here's a way to break your child's bad habit without breaking his spirit.

When we see our kids doing something that isn't good for them, we want to make them stop. Whether it's sucking their thumb or overeating, our immediate reaction is often the harsh approach, "I told you not to do that!" While we might be saying it out of love, our scolding can make our children turn away from us and turn to their habit. You see, habits often develop as a way to deal with an uncomfortable situation.

If your son is biting his nails, instead of shooting a disapproving look, focus on what he's feeling, not what he's doing. Hug him. Ask him what's on his mind. If you get in that habit, you'll help your child break his.

MY THOUGHTS:

_____

_____

_____

BUSINESS TRIPS

"Daddy, what did you bring me?"

If you travel on business a lot, it's important to let your kids know where you are going and that you'll be thinking about them. Before you leave, give them a short geography lesson. Pull out a map and show them your destination. And, sure, you need to call or e-mail them while you're away. But it's also a good idea to bring them a gift home. And guess what? It doesn't have to cost you a dime. You can bring them one of those little bottles of shampoo from your hotel room, or maybe you'll find a historical trinket or a piece of nature like an unusual looking rock, sand from the beach or an autumn leaf.

While your kids will be more excited to see you than what you brought them when you get home, it's just another way to let them know you were thinking of them.

MY THOUGHTS:

_____

_____

_____

PRIVATE DISCIPLINE

Do you like to be corrected in front of other people?

Of course not! We need to remember that when we discipline our children. Correction should always be handled in private. Nothing is more humiliating and degrading to a child than to be disciplined in the grocery store, at school or other public places. Instead, pull your child aside and tell him that you'll handle the matter when you get home. Then follow through.

Even though we might be upset with our child at the time, we still need to honor and respect him by disciplining in private.

MY THOUGHTS:

THE LITTLE THINGS

How can you make your spouse's life easier?

Often, it's the little things that make the biggest impact. Here's an example. A friend of mine said her husband came home from work and sat down beside her on the couch—exhausted. Not really thinking about it, she reached over and took off his shoes for him. No big deal, right? Well, later he told her this: "That was so nice. It was one less thing I had to worry about taking care of."

So do a small favor for your spouse because enough of those little things can help make their life a lot easier.

MY THOUGHTS:

FAMILY MINUTES

HOME BASE

Do you want to have a big influence on your kids' lives?

Make your home the place to be. Kids are influenced by where they spend their time and who they spend it with. And since they're always looking for a cool place to hang out, why not make them feel comfortable at your house? When the kids are little have an area where they can play without having to worry about messing things up. As they get older have sports equipment available and lots of great food in the refrigerator.

By making your home the place to be you'll know where your kids are and whom they're with.

MY THOUGHTS:

AFFECTIONATELY YOURS

Husbands, are you giving your wife the affection she needs?

Think back to your dating days. Remember how you'd shower your wife with compliments, hold her hand and treat her like a queen? So what about now? Men are generally less affectionate than women. And once they're married, the affection they do have can get lost in day-to-day pressures. But listen, most women thrive in an environment of affection.

So, tonight, tell her she's pretty, kiss her on the cheek without expecting anything in return and bring back at least a little of that guy who swept her off her feet.

MY THOUGHTS:

FAMILY MINUTES

VETERANS DAY

Want to know how you can honor your veterans?

Tomorrow is Veterans Day—the day we recognize the military personnel who protect our country. Yet, there's another group who deserves recognition—the military family. Unfortunately, they often go unnoticed. But while Dad is at sea or in the air, Mom becomes a single parent. Or if Mom's in the service and gets new orders, the family moves across the country. And while parades are a great way to celebrate Veterans Day, why not offer free baby-sitting to a military family or give them phone cards for those long separations?

Show your military friends you're grateful for the entire family's sacrifice, and help them find ways to stay connected.

MY THOUGHTS:

_____

_____

_____

HELP SAVE A MARRIAGE

Some caring neighbors helped to save a marriage.

I read an article about a couple who heard their neighbors were divorcing. The couple felt awful. So they asked their friends to attend a marriage conference. Well, the conference was enough to convince their friends to stay married and work through their problems. Just a short time later the couple who had gotten involved heard a knock on the door. It was their neighbors' daughter. She had come to thank them for helping her parents stay together.

If you know someone whose marriage is in trouble, be a real friend. Get involved and help them fight for it.

MY THOUGHTS:

FAMILY MINUTES

BIRTHDAY OUTING

Want to make your daughter or son feel special on their birthday?

Well, go ahead and have a party if that's what they want. But also go on an outing with just Mom, Dad, and the birthday boy or girl. Take them to dinner. Go see a movie, visit the park or do some shopping. Let them help choose the activity. Spending this one-on-one time is especially important if you have more than one child. It gives the guest of honor the chance to have all of your attention. And it gives you the chance to get to know your child better.

Celebrate your child's birthday by reminding them how special they are to you.

MY THOUGHTS:

UNRESOLVED ANGER

What's love's number one enemy?

Marriage expert Gary Smalley says unresolved anger is enemy number one when it comes to love. To handle unresolved anger you need to focus on its root cause—your unfulfilled expectations. Your spouse hasn't done what you expected them to do. You're let down and hurt. You're angry. So tackle this enemy by first identifying your unmet expectations.

Then to get rid of and prevent unresolved anger, it's your responsibility to be direct about your expectations. "Honey, I expected you to invite my parents for dinner, too." Or, "I need you to tell me I look nice when we get dressed up to go out." Be open and direct to avoid unresolved anger.

Resolve your anger and protect your marriage from enemy number one.

MY THOUGHTS:

_____

_____

_____

JUST HAVE FUN

Are your kids overscheduled?

Kids these days are busy. I mean really busy. It's not unusual to have a child in a soccer league, an art course and a language class all at the same time. And while the parents' intentions might be noble, Dr. T. Berry Brazelton and Dr. Stanley I. Greenspan say in their book, *The Irreducible Needs of Children*, that's just too much. They say children need to have time to hang out with their parents doing unorganized things, like throwing the ball around the backyard or going for a walk.

So don't overbook your children. Let them choose one outside activity and make sure they have time to enjoy the carefree days of childhood.

MY THOUGHTS:

_____

_____

_____

GOD BLESS AMERICA

What do you know about the song "God Bless America"?

The same man who wrote it also wrote "White Christmas" and "Puttin' on the Ritz." While he was serving in the Army in 1918, he was inspired to write "God Bless America." But it wasn't released until 1938. And when it was, it became an immediate hit. Well, the writer of this classic is Irving Berlin. He was a Russian immigrant who grew to love the Untied States.

That love inspired a great song we're still singing more than sixty years later.

MY THOUGHTS:

_____

_____

_____

THANKSGIVING DAY PARADE

Have you ever heard of a "balloonatic"?

"Balloonatics" are the people who pull the huge five-story-tall balloons at the Macy's Thanksgiving Day Parade. They make it look so easy that spectators take this amazing feat for granted. Taking things for granted is easy when you only see the end result. What are you taking for granted? A home-cooked meal, good grades from your children or the constant support of your mate?

A simple thank you for those behind-the-scenes efforts is sometimes all it takes to keep your family flying high.

MY THOUGHTS:

_____

_____

_____

3-0-1

If you're having a tough time losing weight, try the 3-0-1 plan.

Being overweight can affect your entire family. It can make you more sluggish and irritable, and you may not have the energy you need to handle the responsibilities of being a mom or dad. A friend of mine said she had tried everything to drop the pounds and finally went to an Overeaters Anonymous meeting. She found out about something called the 3-0-1 plan: three meals a day, no snacks in between, one day at a time. It was just what she needed for structure and to jump start her weight loss.

Now, she's happier, healthier and has more energy for her family.

MY THOUGHTS:

_____

_____

_____

November 17

TRIAL MARRIAGE?

How can you get your marriage off to a good start?

With the divorce rate around 50 percent, the institution of marriage needs all the help it can get. Some people think living together before the wedding is the way to go. In fact, the number of unmarried couples living with each other jumped from 1.6 million in 1980 to almost 4.5 million in 1998. So does it help? The findings from studies done say no. Yale University researchers found that divorce rates for women who live with their future husband before marriage are 80 percent higher than the rates of women who do not.

Studies also show that your marriage will be happier, healthier and stronger if you put off living together until you say, "I do."

MY THOUGHTS:

_____

_____

_____

PARENTING FROM A DISTANCE

Divorced? Live far away from your kids?

If so, here are some ways to help you stay connected. First, be involved in your children's education. Give their teachers self-addressed, stamped envelopes so they can send you updates. Make sure you see report cards and test grades, and e-mail or call as often as you can.

For smaller children, record yourself reading a bedtime story. Make a video of yourself, your office and your pets. Send these tapes to your kids on a regular basis so they can see you and hear you and know how much you love them.

MY THOUGHTS:

_____

_____

_____

FAMILY MINUTES

HONOR

Have you tried just about everything to get your kids to behave?

Maybe you need the honor approach. This is what discipline without honor looks like: a teacher told a fidgety student to sit down. When he refused she stood over him and demanded it. Well, he sat down all right but said this, "I'm sitting on the outside, but I'm standing on the inside." You see, obedience without honor doesn't work in the long run.

What is honor? Basically, honor is three things: treating people as special, doing more than what's expected and having a good attitude.

Once children understand and learn honor, they'll be motivated on their own to behave. It's a principle that will help them for the rest of their lives.

MY THOUGHTS:

HE ALWAYS SAID, "THANKS"

What should we be thankful for this Thanksgiving?

In the midst of a civil war that was tearing his nation apart, Abraham Lincoln found the value in offering "thanks." He said, "Give thanks in everything." Lincoln's point was that true thanksgiving means even giving thanks for difficulties. This Thanksgiving some will have a bountiful holiday—plenty of food, football and fun. Others, however, may be facing a personal Valley Forge filled with suffering and pain. Someone may be without a loved one because of illness, death or military service.

Abraham Lincoln experienced both the good and the extremely difficult. Yet, whatever he faced, he always said, "Thanks."

MY THOUGHTS:

FAMILY MINUTES

GIVING THANKS

Quick! Name three things you're thankful for.

On Thanksgiving Day most of us will pause and give thanks for our blessings. But what about the things to be thankful for the other 364 days of the year? Try this: every morning say out loud three things you're thankful for. I mean it. Do it even if you're having a really rough time in your life. If you think about it, there is always something to be grateful for—your husband, your wife, your children, your health, your faith, the roof over your head, the dollar in your pocket.

Get in the habit of giving thanks, not just on Thanksgiving, but every day.

MY THOUGHTS:

_____

_____

_____

FAMILY EXAMPLE

When you set the table for Thanksgiving, are you also setting a good example?

Most of us think of Thanksgiving as a "family" holiday. Yet, for many people Thanksgiving is a time away from loved ones or time without any family at all. There is the college student far from home for the first time, a lonely widower spending his days in an empty house or the co-worker without any loved ones.

So set an extra place at the table this year, and invite someone to be part of your family for the day. You'll be teaching your kids the true meaning of hospitality. And, you'll be serving up kindness along with your Thanksgiving meal.

MY THOUGHTS:

November 23

SAY CHEESE

If you want Thanksgiving to last all year long, just say "Cheeeeeese."

Family gatherings are the perfect time to make memories. This Thanksgiving snap a picture of every family member and ask them what they're most thankful for. When the pictures come back, mount them in an album with their answer written alongside, and you'll have a "thanks book." Then, when you're all together again next Thanksgiving, take out the "thanks book" and have someone read aloud last year's contributions.

Do this every Thanksgiving, and, who knows, maybe you'll have a new holiday tradition as anticipated as sweet potato pie.

MY THOUGHTS:

FIRST THANKSGIVING

Does your family have a Thanksgiving harvest of its own to celebrate?

When the Indians and Pilgrims sat down together that first Thanksgiving Day, they gave thanks not only for their food, but also for the relationships they shared. Their example is timeless and should be remembered. So when you sit down for turkey and all the trimmings, take stock of the relationships your family has nurtured over the last year. Which ones are stronger? Which ones need to be cultivated? This Thanksgiving enjoy not only the bounty of your current blessings, but make sure you plant relationship seeds for the future. That way, you'll have an even bigger harvest to celebrate next year.

MY THOUGHTS:

_____

_____

_____

November 25

GRANDPARENTING AND YOUTH

If you want to turn back the clock, then hang out with your grandchildren.

That's right. Research shows that grandparents who spend time taking care of their grandchildren actually feel younger and are more active. Those grandparents also say they have a greater purpose in life. You see, when grandparents give their time unselfishly to their grandchildren, an invigorating bond can form. That connection is good for both the grandparent and the grandchildren.

Of course, it can be hectic, and it can be tiring, but what a wonderful and energizing way to turn back the clock.

MY THOUGHTS:

_____

_____

_____

ROUTINE MARRIAGE

Is your marriage just routine?

We all have our routines and that can be a good thing. Routines make our life easier and more predictable—getting to work at the same time, brushing our teeth the same way, getting our groceries at the same place. But routines aren't always great for a marriage. To keep things interesting, you need to shake up your routines every once in a while. Leave your spouse a romantic note, take them on a surprise getaway weekend or wash their car without being asked.

Do the unexpected and give some of your routines a rest.

MY THOUGHTS:

_____

_____

_____

November 27

FAMILY MINUTES

FAITH RENEWAL

Have you been to a worship service lately?

In the days and weeks following the terrorist attacks, houses of worship were packed with people seeking reassurance from God. Many worshippers claimed that just being there gave them peace. That belief, however, is actually backed up by science. A study in the American Medical News found that people who attend church are "both physically healthier and less depressed." It cited benefits for those battling cancer, heart disease and addictions.

So as you seek comfort in trying times, you might want to give church a chance.

MY THOUGHTS:

_____

_____

_____

PILLOW JOURNALS

My wife has a great way to communicate with our kids: she calls it "pillow journals."

To get started she first bought each child a journal and then wrote a note inside. She asked my oldest daughter about her first day of school and told my younger daughter how proud she was of her good behavior. For my son, who's learning to write, she asked a question and made answer boxes for him to check off. Then she laid the journals on the kids' pillows. Later, the children wrote back and put the journals on her pillow. And back and forth they go...

Her loving way of staying in touch lets our kids know how much she cares.

MY THOUGHTS:

LEFTOVERS AGAIN?

Are your kids getting too many leftovers?

I'm not talking about the turkey and dressing sitting in your fridge left over from Thanksgiving. I'm talking about your time. You do the math. Right now, think about all of the things that go into your day—rushing to get ready in the morning, going to work, cleaning the house, cooking dinner, chores in the evening, watching TV. Now, add up how much time you really spend interacting with your kids. What's the grand total?

Are your children getting your best or your leftovers?

MY THOUGHTS:

CHARACTER EDUCATION

Is your family rich in character?

If you were to ask your kids what good character is, what would they say? For that matter, what would you say? Well, here's an easy way to remember a few of the traits that make up good character. Think of the word RICH. R is for respect of self and others. I is for integrity. C is for courage, and H is for honesty.

Talk to your children about what each trait means and how they can put them into action in their daily lives. Encourage them to be RICH in what really matters.

MY THOUGHTS:

_____

_____

_____

WOMEN SMOKERS

Are you willing to give up fourteen years of your life for a cigarette?

A report by the U.S. Surgeon General says that smoking is still a major killer of women. In 1997, approximately 165,000 women died prematurely from diseases linked to smoking. In fact, the surgeon general found that each woman lost an average of fourteen years of her life! That's a high price to pay for a habit.

So if you smoke, do your best to quit. Not only will you be doing it for yourself, but for your family and the other people who love you and want you around for those extra fourteen years.

MY THOUGHTS:

THERMOSTAT OR THERMOMETER

Are you a thermostat or a thermometer in your house?

Some people are thermometers. They merely register what's going on around them. If the situation is tight and pressurized, they register tension and irritability. Others, however, are thermostats. They regulate the atmosphere in their homes. They are the mature ones, the agents of change who never let the situation dictate their behavior.

So when things get hot at your house, instead of reflecting what's going on, you can change things for the better. Be a thermostat—not a thermometer!

MY THOUGHTS:

_____

_____

_____

337   *December 3*

STRONG PARENTING

Do your kids run the show?

Your child is whining to get attention. So you say, "What do you want? Stop whining." Well, there's no incentive for him to stop whining because it worked. He got your attention. Instead say, "I'll listen when you stop whining and you talk in a nice voice." Now you're in control, and he has a reward for changing. The same thing applies when kids don't do their chores. Instead of nagging, say, "Only the kids who finish their chores get allowance."

Try telling your children what you will do instead of always telling them what to do.

MY THOUGHTS:

_____

_____

_____

ARGUMENT CURFEW

If you want a new way to avoid arguments with your spouse, then synchronize your watches.

Soon after my wife and I were married, we made a discovery. It seemed like we did our arguing at night when we were tired and irritable from a long day. So we set a curfew on serious discussions: nine o'clock is the limit. We have found that it really works. Now when we start to get into a heavy talk after our curfew, we remind each other that it's late, we're not going to resolve anything tonight and we can talk about it tomorrow.

And do you know what? The next morning we're refreshed and can talk about it calmly. We may even decide it wasn't that important to begin with.

MY THOUGHTS:

_____

_____

_____

December 5

FAMILY MINUTES

MAIL A MEMORY

If you have loved ones who can't make it home for the holidays, then serve them memories instead.

Those far from home probably long for the smell of a flour-dusted kitchen or the hearty flavor of a roasted turkey. So mail them a memory. One mom sent her college daughter the same Thanksgiving bouquet that sat on their table at home. A man received pictures of a long-ago Thanksgiving dinner when he was a boy. And a military friend stationed far from home recalled his mom's cooking by reading her recipe cards as he ate his dinner from a can.

So, if you won't be able to make memories with your loved ones during the holidays—mail them instead.

MY THOUGHTS:

PROTECTING YOUR MARRIAGE

Are you protecting your marriage?

To keep your marriage strong, certain aspects have to be protected. Protect your time. Make sure you carve out time for just you and your spouse. Hire a baby-sitter or trade baby-sitting time with another family so you can get out. Protect your heart. Keep your romantic thoughts focused on your mate. Avoid situations and people that might tempt you. Finally, protect your marriage with words. Kind words can make your marriage stronger, but harsh words can make it vulnerable to attack.

It's up to you to protect your marriage.

MY THOUGHTS:

HELP WANTED

Are you a single parent looking for help?

Raising your kids alone can be a tough and lonely road. Well, help could be just around the corner. These days many churches have specific ministries for single parents. They provide childcare, mentors for kids and classes for handling the special challenges of single parenting. They also offer fellowship with other parents who are in the same boat and support from older church members who want to reach out to families doing the best they can.

So if you're a single parent who needs help, step out and look for it. It could be just around the corner.

MY THOUGHTS:

MARRIAGE DIET

Does your marriage need to go on a diet?

In other words, do you have heavy, serious conversations every day? To make your marriage lighter have a weekly meeting. Instead of talking about issues every time they come up, you should write them down and save a list for the time you've agreed to. When your meeting does finally roll around, go over your list. You may find that what had bothered you earlier isn't a big deal any more. Waiting also gives you time to think about the best way to bring up a matter.

Just like a diet, it will take determination. But the results will be worth it.

MY THOUGHTS:

GIFT OF THE MAGI

Do you know what the greatest gift is?

The writer O. Henry tells the story of Della and Jim, a young couple madly in love but too poor to buy Christmas gifts for each other. So, Della goes out and sells her beautiful, long hair and then buys Jim a chain for his treasured pocket watch. Later that evening, Jim comes home. He stares in shock at Della's cropped hair. As he sits speechless, Della gives him the watch chain. He then silently hands Della a box. Inside is a lovely set of combs for her hair. Jim had bought them by selling his watch.

Each had sacrificed their most treasured possession. So what is the greatest gift? Love.

MY THOUGHTS:

_____

_____

_____

THREE WISHES

Want a fun way to find out what your children are thinking?

To get a glimpse inside your children's minds, play "three wishes." It's as simple as it sounds. Ask them to tell you what they would ask for if they had three wishes. When they answer, talk about what they chose, even if it's something as basic as a new dog. You might find out that your children have hopes and dreams you can help them achieve. Or, you might learn that there's something painful in their lives they need your help changing.

So if you've been wishing for a way to get your children to open up, give it a try.

MY THOUGHTS:

_____

_____

_____

RAISING BOYS RIGHT

What are the two primary ways fathers influence their sons?

In his book *Bringing Up Boys*, Dr. James Dobson says the best way to transfer our values to our children is through modeling and instruction. First is modeling. Anyone with boys knows that they often imitate their father. So, Dads, if you frequently speak harshly to your wife, your sons will probably treat women disrespectfully. If you abuse alcohol, your kids may follow in your footsteps. But if you're patient, kind and self-controlled, your sons will also likely be these things.

The second way a father can influence his boys is through specific instruction. And one of the most important things a father can teach his son is how to treat women—like standing up for them at the table or opening their door. Let your son also know that he should never hit a girl. And, tell him not to take anything that doesn't belong to him, especially the moral purity of a woman.

MY THOUGHTS:

_____

_____

_____

RECEIVING

"Don't you remember I told you not to get me anything?"

For many of us, it's easier to give than to receive. We just aren't comfortable accepting gifts or gestures of appreciation. So to deflect that attention, we say things like, "You shouldn't have spent so much money on me." And even though our intentions might be humble ones, our actions belittle the generosity of the giver. So the next time you're on the receiving end, no matter how uncomfortable you feel, allow the other person to enjoy their giving experience.

Just say "thanks."

MY THOUGHTS:

_____

_____

_____

FAMILY MINUTES

SUPER KID

It's one of your children's turn to be Super Kid.

Kathy, a single mom of four, sent me this great idea. Her kids take turns being Super Kid for a week. Super Kid gets privileges like riding in the front seat and choosing the first cupcake. Kathy says this prevents bickering since the others know their turn is coming. Super Kid also gets extra time with Mom: going out for ice cream or staying up late together. And to prevent selfishness, at the end of the week, Super Kid points out good behavior in his siblings, encouraging a positive attitude.

We all like a chance to feel like we are something super.

MY THOUGHTS:

NEGATIVES IN MARRIAGE

Do you know the four habits that can destroy your marriage?

According to Scott M. Stanley and his colleagues, authors of the book *A Lasting Promise—Fighting for Your Marriage*, four patterns destroy marriages: escalation, invalidation, negative interpretations and withdrawal.

Escalation turns simple discussions into a heated arguments. Invalidation means putting down the thoughts, feelings or character of the other spouse. Negative interpretations happen when one spouse assumes the worst in the other's intentions or motivations. The withdrawal pattern involves leaving important discussions or avoiding them completely.

So keep your marriage positive and avoid these four destructive communication patterns.

MY THOUGHTS:

EVERY LITTLE BIT HELPS

Heard about the chewing gum diet?

A study shows that chewing gum every day can help you lose almost a pound a month! Isn't that amazing how one little thing can make such a big difference? Now apply that to your home life. Most of us think that to please our spouse or kids we have to do things in a big way. So we put things off until we have time for something special. Why not start small? Instead of saving up our expressions of love for a big moment, share them bit by bit. Instead of waiting for a major outing with your kids, just take time to play with them.

Like the chewing gum diet, those little moments add up to something big.

MY THOUGHTS:

Holiday

SECERT SANTA

Want to make someone's holiday season?

A friend of mine is a kind of secret Santa. She drives around her neighborhood and finds people who are brightening things up with a nice yard display or beautiful lights. Then, she later goes quietly back and leaves them a note in their mailbox. In the note she thanks them for going to the trouble of making their home festive and welcoming. This anonymous thanking can work in other ways too. Maybe you know of someone who helps out in a soup kitchen or donates gifts to needy children. Write them an anonymous note and let them know their kind deeds are appreciated.

During a season of giving, the greatest gift to receive may be encouragement.

MY THOUGHTS:

FAMILY MINUTES

FREE GIFT

Want to give a holiday present that won't cost a penny?

With as many activities as some nursing homes have, they can still be lonely places. Activities are no substitute for hugs, kisses and conversations from friends and family. So as the holiday season approaches, give the gift of your time to someone you love or the gift of friendship to someone who doesn't have family nearby.

Spending a small amount of your time visiting someone in a nursing home won't cost you anything, and it may put a smile on a face and joy in a heart.

MY THOUGHTS:

WHAT WIVES WISH...

Men, do you really know your wife?

The French say, "Vive le difference!" In other words, thank goodness for the differences between men and women. But the differences that make marriage so exciting can also make it challenging. In Dr. James Dobson's book, *What Wives Wish Their Husbands Knew about Women*, he addresses things such as loneliness in marriage, finances and health issues that can affect relationships.

Take the time to find out what wives wish their husbands knew about them. You might realize how much you have to learn about your wife.

MY THOUGHTS:

THE PERFECT CHRISTMAS?

Do the holidays at your house have to be perfect?

This may sound familiar. The gifts have to be wrapped just so. The decorations have to be hung on the tree like this. The Christmas cookies must have this color icing.

The holidays can bring on a lot of extra pressure—if you let them. So avoid that intensity and be flexible. If traditions turn out a little differently this year, it's okay. If the kids don't hang the ornaments on the tree just right, let it go. Enjoy your children, family and friends in the spirit of the season.

In your celebration, forget perfection.

MY THOUGHTS:

GIVE 'TIL IT FEELS GOOD

Is your "help radar" in good condition or does it need a tune-up?

Here's an example of a fine-tuned "help radar." It just so happens to belong to my wife. We have an elderly neighbor. Of course if she asks me to take out the garbage or wash her car, I'm there in a second. So my help radar is working. But my wife's is automatic. She instinctively sees beyond the obvious. Just last week she went over to our neighbor's and volunteered to take her grocery shopping and run errands for her. My wife's "help radar" saw through to the next level of need.

To some helping others comes naturally. But for the rest of us it's time for a tune-up.

MY THOUGHTS:

_____

_____

_____

CHRISTMAS GIVING

Christmas: peace and plenty, or longsuffering and loneliness?

For many, the joys of the season are plentiful. But for others it can be filled with sadness and loneliness. There is the wife who just lost her husband of forty years; the spouse who is in the middle of a terrible divorce; the parents whose rebellious child won't be home for Christmas. If your emotional stocking is full, your face is lit up with joy and the children are all nestled around the fireplace, remember, this is a season for sharing your time and giving words of hope.

Think of someone who is hurting and pray for God's peace.

MY THOUGHTS:

DO YOU BELIEVE?

If you don't believe in Santa Claus, you might after you read this.

In fourth-century Turkey, a wealthy teenager heard about a poor and starving family. If the family did not get some money fast the children would have to be sold into slavery. So, late one night, the teen went to the family's house and tossed a bag of gold coins through the window...and that was just the beginning of his kindness. He eventually became a priest and a bishop, known for his generosity to the poor and needy. As he aged, he grew a long white beard and had a big belly beneath his red robe. Ring a bell? His name was Saint Nicholas—better known as Saint Nick.

So, you see, there really is a Santa Claus.

MY THOUGHTS:

CHRISTMAS TRADITIONS

There are some things that never change.

During the holidays we can take comfort in the familiar—traditions that strengthen our family bond. In my home, you will always find the kids making cookies—and me eating them. On Christmas Eve we share the story of the first Christmas. And as my children grow and have their own families, they'll have these traditions to hold onto.

So in the busyness of the holiday season, create your own traditions. Because even when all of the other presents have been forgotten, traditions are a gift you can open again and again.

MY THOUGHTS:

ONE SOLITARY LIFE

Who is the greatest man that ever lived?

Born in an obscure village to a peasant woman, he worked in a carpenter shop until he was 30 years old. Then, for three years, he was an itinerant preacher. He never set foot inside a big city, never wrote a book or held office. He did none of the things that usually accompany greatness. While just a young man, popular opinion turned against him. He was nailed to a cross, died, but then rose again. Twenty centuries later he is the central figure for much of the human race.

All the armies that ever marched, all the navies that ever sailed, and all the kings that ever reigned, put together, have not affected mankind as powerfully as this "One Solitary Life."

MY THOUGHTS:

JIMMY STEWART MOVIES

Did you see *It's a Wonderful Life* this year?

That holiday classic is one of Jimmy Stewart's best movies. But he has other hits that are great family movies, too. Here are a few of them: *You Can't Take It with You* is a comedy that talks about what's really important in life. *Mr. Smith Goes to Washington* has Jimmy Stewart as a kind and courageous politician. And, *Shop around the Corner* is a romance fit for all ages.

So don't wait until next Christmas to watch a Jimmy Stewart movie. Check out these other films the whole year through.

MY THOUGHTS:

_____

_____

_____

GREAT EXPECTATIONS

Do you have big plans for your children?

Do you dream of your children becoming great athletes or straight-A students? Although it's normal to have dreams for our children, when reality doesn't measure up, it's time to let go and love. That's right, let go of the expectations and love your children unconditionally. Accept them for who they are. Show them with words and actions that you love them because they are your child not because of what they can do or accomplish.

So change your focus from their shortcomings and your dreams to the gifts that will help make their dreams come true.

MY THOUGHTS:

CHRISTMAS CLUB

Already making plans for next Christmas?

Sure, you just wrapped up Christmas a few days ago. But it's time to start thinking about next year. Why?—to save you from debt. The average American family spends about $500 on Christmas gifts. Of course, if you can afford it, it's great to be generous. But if you're buying on credit, I have an idea for you. Starting January 1, save one dollar every day. And not just in theory, but actually take a dollar from your wallet and put it in a designated place. Then by next Christmas, you'll have $358.

Start planning now for a peaceful and debt-free Christmas.

MY THOUGHTS:

_____

_____

_____

CONNECTED KIDS

Are you really connected to your kids?

Here's a short test for you, Mom and Dad. What's your child's favorite TV show? How about their favorite movie, musician and magazine? What sites do they visit on the Internet? Name their three best friends. Name their favorite teacher—their least favorite teacher. So how are you doing? Could you answer all of those questions? Could you answer even half of them? The point is, to be connected to our kids, we have to enter their world. We need to know what they like, who they like and what has their attention.

So get involved. Start asking questions and get connected.

MY THOUGHTS:

_____

_____

_____

HOLIDAY HUMILITY

The holidays are almost over, and our children will soon head back to school.

Classmates will undoubtedly ask, "What did you get for Christmas?" While it's a natural question, is it a necessary one? Some children may not have gotten many presents. Maybe their family couldn't afford them. Or, maybe they decided to focus less on the material aspects of the holidays. Either way, this is a situation we can use to teach our children a couple of lessons. First, if they did get a lot of gifts, we can tell them how bragging not only makes them look bad, but it may cause others to feel even worse. And by not asking the question, they might prevent hurt feelings.

Holiday giving is wonderful. But holiday humility is even better.

MY THOUGHTS:

_____

_____

_____

RESOLUTIONS

How many New Year's resolutions have you ever kept?

Most of us have grand plans for changes in the New Year. We confidently take on losing weight, better budgeting and not yelling at our kids. And, yes, we can do it...until about January 3. So this time, target just one specific step that will get you to your goal. Instead of "lose twenty pounds," try "walk fifteen minutes every day." I know, I know, that sounds like nothing. But the key here is that you're focusing on something that's realistic.

So pick one—yes, one goal—and start with the first step. Who knows, maybe you'll keep that resolution and then some.

MY THOUGHTS:

Mark Merrill is the father of three young children. That alone could provide sufficient experience for any insightful book on the family. But Mark is more than a husband and father, and his family perspective is shaped by more than practical first-hand knowledge.

He is also the founder and president of Family First, a widely respected non-profit research and communications organization dedicated to strengthening the family. As an energetic advocate for the family, he speaks to civic, business and religious organizations on the importance of strong families in today's culture.

Mark is the host of *Family Minute with Mark Merrill*, a national daily radio program, and he has also promoted family awareness on other radio programs including the Canadian Broadcasting Network, NPR and CBS Radio. His comments and writings have appeared in numerous publications including *USA Today*, *the Washington Times* and *Sports Illustrated*.

Before founding Family First in 1991, Mark practiced law in Florida for seven years. He received his Juris Doctor degree from the University of Florida.

Mark, his wife Susan, and their three young children — Megan, Emily and Mark, Jr. — live in Tampa.

FAMILY FIRST

A re you looking for more *Family Minutes* wisdom? Then be sure to sign up for the free daily e-mail at **FamilyMinute.net**.

Family Minutes is a production of Family First, a non-profit organization dedicated to strengthening the family. Family First has a variety of resources available (many of them free) at **FamilyFirst.net**.

For more information, or to request a Family First representative to speak at your event, contact us at:

FAMILY FIRST
P. O. Box 2882
Tampa, Florida 33601
1-800-956-8300
e-mail: info@familyfirst.net
